Chinese Kung Fu

Wushu, the Chinese martial art form known as kung fu in the West, embodies traditional Chinese culture and reflects the self defense and fitness practices of the Chinese people. The core philosophy of wushu is drawn from Confucian, Taoist and Buddhist principles and the Eastern philosophy that humans are an integral part of nature. In this illustrated introduction Wang Guangxi discusses the theory, schools, weapons and development of this distinctive and captivating branch of Chinese culture from ancient times to the present day, including its representation in literature and film.

Introductions to Chinese Culture

The thirty volumes in the Introductions to Chinese Culture series provide accessible overviews of particular aspects of Chinese culture written by a noted expert in the field concerned. The topics covered range from architecture to archaeology, from mythology and music to martial arts. Each volume is lavishly illustrated in full color and will appeal to students requiring an introductory survey of the subject, as well as to more general readers.

Wang Guangxi

CHINESE KUNG FU

CAMBRIDGE
UNIVERSITY PRESS

CAMBRIDGE UNIVERSITY PRESS
Cambridge, New York, Melbourne, Madrid, Cape Town,
Singapore, São Paulo, Delhi, Tokyo, Mexico City

Cambridge University Press
The Edinburgh Building, Cambridge CB2 8RU, UK

Published in the United States of America by Cambridge University Press,
New York

www.cambridge.org
Information on this title: www.cambridge.org/9780521186643

Originally published by China Intercontinental Press as
Chinese Kung Fu (9787508513171) in 2010

© China Intercontinental Press 2010

This updated edition is published by Cambridge University Press
with the permission of China Intercontinental Press under
the China Book International programme 🌀.

For more information on the China Book International programme, please visit
http://www.cbi.gov.cn/wisework/content/10005.html

Cambridge University Press retains copyright in its own contributions
to this updated edition

© Cambridge University Press 2012

First published 2012

Printed and bound in China by C&C Offset Printing Co., Ltd

A catalogue record for this publication is available from the British Library

ISBN 978-0-521-18664-3 Paperback

Contents

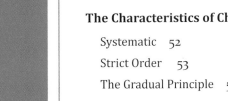

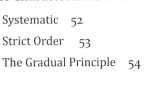

Foreword

Wushu, the Chinese martial art form known as kung fu in the West, is an important part of Chinese culture. It reflects the character of Chinese people, and applies their theories and principles to combat. It differs in many ways from other forms of combat, such as boxing, karate and Muay Thai. Wushu strikes a unique balance between hard and soft, and between extrinsic and intrinsic values, and can demonstrate the potential beauty and elegance of the human figure. Rooted in ancient Chinese philosophers' understanding of life and the universe, wushu is much more than just a combat technique.

Wushu, which ultimately aims to improve one's health and self-defense skills, begins with the mind. While demonstrating martial art movements, an expert's mind remains calm and neutral. The energy is dynamic on the outside but calm and focused on the inside. Wushu does not encourage

Stretched out view of copper pot with scenes of land- and water-based warfare. Warring States Period, Chengdu, Sichuan province.

fighting or bravery; instead, peace and quiet are considered its goals.

Having maintained its strength and vitality for so long, some believe wushu to be the epitome of traditional Chinese culture and to be representative of China's national spirit.

The Origins of Martial Arts

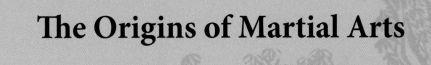

The term "wushu" literally translates as "martial art," and since 1949 wushu has been the name for the modern exhibition and full-contact sport that is judged according to a set of aesthetic criteria. Outside China, it is often referred to as kung fu, although in Chinese this term can also be used in contexts completely unrelated to martial arts. Wushu is a more precise term for general martial arts. Its origins are rooted in ancient tribal wars. An excerpt from *The Book of Poetry* dates martial arts to the Spring and Autumn Period (770 BC– 476 BC). Passages in the *Zhuangzi* text record more than 3,000 of King Zhao's swordsmen (late Qin Dynasty) fighting day and night without growing tired. During the Han Dynasty (202 BC–AD 220), the practice of martial arts made remarkable progress. Many paintings and stone sculptures from that period have been unearthed in Henan, some of which involve swords, spears and lances while others demonstrate separate "solo" and "sparring" elements.

Mirror design depicting a fight between a man and an animal. Qin Dynasty (221–206), Yunmeng, Hunan province.

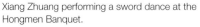

Xiang Zhuang performing a sword dance at the Hongmen Banquet.

The drawing portrays the famous story of Hongmen Banquet. In 206 BC, two states, Chu and Han, clashed after the Qin Dynasty ended. Liu Bang, King of Han state, went to Hongmen to meet Xiang Yu, King of Chu state. During the banquet, Xiang Zhuang performed the sword dance as a cover for his attempt on Liu Bang's life.

Martial arts and hunting scenes. Hollow brick relief. Eastern Han Dynasty (25–220), Zhengzhou, Henan province.

Qigong Jade Inscription.

Qigong Jade Inscription
The jade column with twelve sides dates from the early Warring States period and is kept in the Tianjin History Museum. Forty-five engraved characters describe a method of Qigong practice similar to Zhoutiangong. It is the earliest record of Qigong ever found in China.

This inscription translates as, "When exercising *Qi* energy, one must take a deep breath and store more energy to enable one's *Qi* to extend to the lower part of one's body. When *Qi* moves below the waist, one must stop to make *Qi* sink. Then breathe out the *Qi* in reverse direction, like grass in a bud growing upward. With mutual movement and exchange, if one exercises *Qi* along this direction, one can live longer; if against this direction, one will die."

Taoism formed after the Spring and Autumn Period. The famous Chinese philosopher Laozi advocated the "renewal of oneself while embracing perfect peace" and the "unity of body and mind while concentrating on breathing." Zhuangzi proposed the idea of "exhaling the old and inhaling the new." The *Xingqi Yupei Ming*, or the *Qi Circulation Inscription*, which dates from the Warring States Period (475–221 BC), records the *qi*-promoting method (*qi* is usually translated as energy). Laozi and Zhuangzi's theory of cultivating *qi* combined the theory of yin-and-yang with the theory of the five elements: metal, wood, water, fire and earth. This became the training basis for the meditation of wushu. Some of Laozi's philosophical theories, such as restricting action through silence and conquering the unyielding with the yielding, were absorbed by various styles of wushu and are considered the principles of the internal elements of martial arts.

An example of armed versus unarmed combat. Stone relief, Han Dynasty, Nanyang, Henan province.

Cultivating extrinsic and intrinsic values and unifying the body and soul are fundamental characteristics of wushu. Martial arts emphasize the importance of *qi*, while martial artists are trained to transfer the potential energy in their bodies and achieve the goal of "mind leading *qi* and *qi* promoting strength." During the Song (960–1279) and Yuan (1271–1368) Dynasties, martial arts began to incorporate *qi*-promoting techniques. Shaolin kung fu matured by the end of the Ming Dynasty (1368–1644) and the Wudang styles grew out of the same period; both are seen as important stages in the historical development of martial arts.

The Principles of Wushu

Tiger-shaped stone, from *China's Scenery* by Okada Gyokuzan, published in 1802.

Li Guang, a famous general of the Western Han Dynasty (BC 206–AD 25), shoots an arrow into a stone in the shape of a crouching tiger while on a night patrol.

Whether a person has reached the highest level in martial arts is measured by four aspects: force, fist position, strength and psychology. Together, these four aspects make up an organic whole and embody martial arts at the highest level. For a kung fu master, his force should have the quality of both pliability and hardness; his fist position should be nimble but with a clumsy outward appearence; his strength should be able to hit people by his will; and his mind should be prepared to fight, but not act in anger.

Being able to determine an appropriate balance between hard and soft and between external and internal forces is required for all styles of martial arts. Force is linked to the concept of "yang," while "yin" is linked to the concept of mercy. In Chinese wushu,

The *Sixth Patriarch Cutting Bamboo*, by Liang Kai.
Southern Song Dynasty (1127–1279)

Huineng was the sixth patriarch of Buddhism in ancient
China. This drawing makes use of bold lines and a simple,
unsophisticated style.

there is no pure "hard fist" position, nor a pure "yielding soft fist" position. If the fist is too hard, then the strength will be exhausted; if it is too soft, the strength will be too weak. Both have obvious drawbacks. Only a balance of the two can allow the fist to switch smoothly and harmoniously between the ways of yin and yang.

The phrase "cats hide their claws" comes from the philosophy of Laozi, and implies that the smartest thing can seem simple. Monks use this term to explain how high-level martial arts are practical, as opposed to complicated or beautiful. An important discipline of wushu is that a beautiful thing may not be practical, and often a practical thing is not beautiful. The smart object may not be better than the simple object, and most simple things can exceed smart things. Therefore, the mystery of wushu does not lie within tangible skills because the greatest skills are intangible.

Martial artists use qi (the functional activities of the body) to create the force to hit an adversary.

This can be broken down into several steps: "strength comes from will," "force derives from mind" and "fist works as desired." The idea is to transfer the energy from one's body by will power, focus one's strength on one particular point, and then release that force.

Martial artists aspire to fight well without being influenced by anger. Laozi said that a good fighter was never angry. A man who is easily angered will never be a good fighter. Therefore, those learning martial arts must learn to control and adjust their moods: they should remain calm when they meet with enemies and remain undaunted in the face of perils.

An understanding of the concepts of hardness and softness together with the ability to control one's emotions are essential for those wishing to reach the highest levels. These aspects are the pillars that underpin wushu.

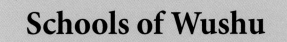

Schools of Wushu

China is a vast country with a long history. Its physical and human geography are highly complex. The levels of economic and cultural development vary from region to region, and a number of small regions with distinct cultural characteristics have formed such as the Central Plains, Qi-Lu, Jing-Chu, Guan-Long, Wu Yue, Ba-Shu, Lingnan, the southern Fujian culture and the emerging cultural areas in Beijing and Shanghai.

Wushu varies from region to region, and distinct differences are apparent between the major wushu schools.

Huang Zongxi, one of the foremost Chinese scholars and reformers of the early Qing dynasty (1644–1911) proposed the idea of "Neijia" (internal) and "Waijia" (external) styles. He classified the more attack-minded schools (for example, Shaolinquan) as the external type, and those that put more emphasis on defense (for example, Wudangquan) as the internal type. The external type is considered the tougher and stronger, while the internal type is considered the gentler.

Over time, the different regional cultures led to seven identifiable families of wushu. Each focuses on one or more general principles, and has a number of schools. The seven major families are:

1: Shaolin: centered on Songshan Shaolin Temple and widely practiced in northern China.

2: Wudang: based on Jing-Chu culture, centered on Wudang Mountain in Hubei province and practiced in Hubei, Henan, Jiangsu, Sichuan and Shanghai.

Portrait of Huang Zongxi

Huang Zongxi, also known as Huang Lizhou, put forward the concept of hitting vital points for the first time.

3: Emei: based on Ba-shu culture, centered on Emei Mountain in Sichuan province and practiced in southern China.

4: Nanquan: based on southern Fujian and Lingnan cultures, centered on Quanzhou and the Pearl River Delta and practiced in southern China.

5: Xingyiquan: based on Shanxi, Yan-Zhao and Central Plains cultures, centered on Shanxi, Hebei and Henan and practiced throughout the entire country.

6: Taijiquan: based on Central Plains and Beijing culture, centered on Henan and Beijing and practiced throughout the entire country.

7: Baguazhang: based on Beijing culture, centered on Beijing and practiced throughout the entire country.

The Shaolin, Wudang and Emei families are older, while the Xingyi, Taiji and Bagua families formed later. These later families first became popular in northern China. Martial arts practitioners consider Wudang, Xingyi, Taiji and Bagua the four major internal schools.

Shaolinquan Family

Many people believe that kung fu originates from Shaolin. The magnificent Shaolin Temple located at the foot of Mount Song at Dengfeng in Henan Province is the cradle of Shaolin kung fu. In Taoism, Mount Song is one of the Five Sacred Mountains.

According to one historical record, the Shaolin Temple was built around AD 495 during the Taihe era of the Northern Wei Dynasty. Other sources suggest that it was built at an earlier date, and some believe that the first Indian Buddhist monk to live there was Gunabhadra (394–468). Bodhidharma (unknown–536) is also said to have once visited the Shaolin Temple; one story says he gazed at a wall in the Shaolin Monastery for nine years.

Songshan Shaolin Temple

Shaolinquan was the physical manifestation of the wisdom of the monks of the temple, secular wushu masters and army generals and soldiers. According to archaeological records, kung fu in the Central Plains developed during the Eastern (206 BC–AD 25) and Western Han (25–220) Dynasties, and shaolinquan developed from this. The monks of the Shaolin Temple were mainly from the Central Plains, so some monks had already learned kung fu before entering the temple. These monks then taught others after entering the temple. The Shaolin Temple always attempted to improve its own teachings by observing and learning from those of nearby monasteries.

At the end of the Sui Dynasty (581–618), thirteen monks helped Li Shimin (599–649), emperor of the Tang Dynasty, defeat Wang Shichong. This helped to popularize Shaolinquan. During the Five Dynasties Period (907–960), the Shaolin monk Fuju invited eighteen martial arts masters to help improve Shaolinquan. Fuju absorbed the best martial art techniques from the others and compiled the *Shaolin Quan*. During the Jin and

Bhadra
During the rule of the Emperor Xiaowen of the Northern Wei Dynasty, Bhadra came to China from India to spread Buddhism. After the Northern Wei Dynasty relocated its capital to Luoyang, the emperor built a temple for him there - the Shaolin Temple. He was the founder and the first abbot of Shaolin Temple. He translated scriptures such as Huayan, Nirvanasutra, Vimalakirti Sutra, and Ten Stages Sutra.

Bodhidharma
Bodhidharma was from southern India. As a Brahman, he claimed to be the twenty-eighth Zen Buddhism patriarch and the earliest Chinese patriarch of Zen Buddhism. Thus Chinese Zen Buddhism is also known as Dharma Zen. He sailed to Guangzhou during the reign of Emperor Wu of Liang, of the Southern Dynasty, who believed in Buddhism. Dharma went to Jianye, the capital of the Southern Dynasty, to meet the emperor but they could not reach an agreement. He therefore sailed north to Luoyang, the capital of the Northern Wei, and the Shaolin Temple. Legend says that he stared at a wall there for nine years, and handed down his mantle and alms bowl to Hui Ke. In the third year (536) of Tianping period of the Eastern Wei Dynasty, he died in Luohe, and was buried on Mount Xiong'er.

Yuan dynasties (1115–1234), the Shaolin monk Jueyuan, Li Sou (a famous martial artist from Lanzhou) and Bai Yufeng (a famous martial artist from Luoyang who entered the temple and took the name Qiu Yue Chan Shi) created more than seventy Shaolin techniques. The style gradually developed and matured during the Sui, Tang, Jin and Yuan dynasties.

By the Ming and Qing dynasties, it was well known around the world. During the Jiajing period of the Ming Dynasty (1522–1566), the Shaolin Temple sent more than eighty monks to defeat Japanese pirates. In the fortieth year of the Jiajing reign (1561), the Ming general Yu Dayou (1504–1580) went to the Shaolin Temple to teach cudgel-fighting skills. After this, Shaolin monks switched from cudgel fighting to fist fighting. At the end of the Ming Dynasty, Shaolin monk Hong Ji learned outstanding spear-fighting skills from Liu Dechang.

During the late Ming and early Qing eras, Shaolinquan absorbed the best features of many northern schools, for example the cudgel-fighting skills of Fujian province and the spear-fighting skills of Sichuan province. The broad and extensive Shaolin family was formed, and finally

Bodhidharma sailing across a river on reed stalk (left)

It is said that this was originally drawn by a monk who had gone mad.

Drawing of Shaolinquan.

This is a mural painting of Baiyi Hall, part of the Shaolin Temple. Known as 'Chui Pu', and drawn during the early Qing Dynasty, it shows features of Shaolinquan.

achieved a respected position in the wushu community. As Shaolinquan became more famous, many schools in northern China proclaimed themselves part of the same family. In this way, the family covered nearly all the Chinese martial schools of the northern region and Shaolinquan became the general term for wushu.

Many techniques currently prevalent in the north, such as Meihua Quan ("plum-blossom fist"), and Paoquan ("canon fist"), all belong to the Shaolin family. Every movement has its own independent fist forms and techniques. At present, the Shaolin Temple has 371 different forms, including 234 varying types of fist fighting and 137 ways to use weapons. It is also said that Shaolinquan has 72 secret forms.

Shaolinquan is known for being powerful and strong, and the men from the Central Plains are renowned for their height, strength and the force of their fists.

Portrait of Zhang Sanfeng, Ming Dynasty.

This is the earliest known portrait of Zhang Sanfeng, and was a gift from him to the Li family. Li Wenzhong, a member of the Li family, was a nephew of Zhu Yuanzhang and one of the founding fathers of the Ming Dynasty. The Li family was known for its hospitality, and Zhang Sanfeng visited the Li family occasionally.

Shaolinquan is also simple and modest: it is based on the practicality of fighting. Shaolin fist fighting is described as "fighting along a single straight line". According to this method, one should use maximum strength to defend one's body. Shaolinquan requires all strikes to be executed within a small area, and the distance between two combatants should be no more than a few steps.

Today's martial arts were largely shaped and cradled by the Shaolin Temple. Shaolinquan is considered the grandfather of all Asian martial arts. Its keystone is the integration of fighting and the philosophy of Buddhism. The original aim of the Shaolin monks was to protect the temple and Buddhism. Shaolin monks were required to practice meditation, an integral part of Buddhist practice. Dhyanna was an Indian form of Buddhist meditation, which emphasized seated meditation to help bring about enlightenment in its practitioners. This may be a reason why the Shaolin Temple produces so many wushu masters.

The Shaolin family has strong links with other families, and has also had a great influence on the formation of Emei, Nanquan, Xingyi and Taiji.

Wudangquan Family

Shaolin and Wudang are considered the two dominant schools in wushu, and each is seen to have its own unique merits.

Located in the north-western region of Hubei province, the Wudang Mountains cover an area of more than 30 square kilometers. The tallest point peak, Heavenly Pillar Peak, rises 1612 meters above sea level. The natural scenery of Wudang Mountain is powerful and magnificent. It was the sacred Taoist Holy Land in China

The Taoists of the Wudang Mountains began practicing fist-fighting a long time ago. The Qing scholar Huang Zongxi believed Wudangquan was created by Zhang Sanfeng, but there is no historical record to verify this claim. According to historical records, Zhang Sanfeng was a Taoist of the Quanzhen sect, and lived during the late Yuan and early Qing Dynasties. He practiced martial arts in the Wudang Mountains, but knew nothing about fist-fighting techniques.

Portrait of Zhao Kuangyin, the first emperor of the Northern Song Dynasty.

Zhao Kuangyin (927–976) was the son of a general. Wudangquan and Shaolinquan both have Changquan forms named after this emperor. It is said such forms were created by him.

The Wudang sect is secretive about its techniques and has always selected its students very carefully. Wudangquan has therefore never spread far. It was taught until the late Ming and early Qing Dynasties. In Ningbo, Zhejiang province, Wudang masters such as Zhang Songxi, Ye Jinquan, Shan Sinan and Wang Zhengnan emerged. Huang Baijia (born 1634), the son of Huang Zongxi, was a student of Wang Zhengnan. It is believed that Zhang Songxi taught Wudangquan in Sichuan province. The Songxi Neijiaquan, Wudang Neijiaquan and Zimu Nanquan styles found in Chengdu and Nanchong, Sichuan province, all belong to the Wudang family. During the Guangxu period in the late Qing Dynasty (1875–1908), Taoists set up a school and taught students in Jiangning (now Nanjing City), Jiangsu province. Wudangquan is still popular in Sichuan and Jiangsu provinces. To date, Wudang Taoists still maintain the tradition of practicing martial arts.

It is estimated that there are now more than sixty varieties of Wudangquan, including Taiyi Wuxing Quan ("Taiyi five element form"), Changquan ("long list") and Liuye Miansi ("palm"). There are also many other styles that make use of weapons. The family includes the well known Xuanwu Quan, Mianzhang Quan ("soft palm"), Huzhua Quan ("tiger claw"), Dilong Quan, Hongyuan Quan and Taijiquan.

Taoism emphasizes quietness, passivity and good health, and Wudangquan therefore pays the same attention to defensive as offensive skills. The aim is to gain mastery by striking only after the enemy has struck.

The Wudang family formed in the late Ming and early Qing dynasties, around the same time as the Shaolin family.

Emeiquan Family

The Emeiquan family is centered on Mount Emei, in Sichuan province. It is the second-largest family in south China after Nanquan.

The stunning Mount Emei is situated in the middle of Sichuan province. Enriched with the spirit of the mountains and rivers, it is one of the most famous mountains in Chinese Buddhism. Legend says it is the ritual site of Samantabhadra.

It is thought by some that Taoists and monks on Mount Emei have a long martial arts tradition, but there are only a few historical records to prove this. In the mid-Ming Dynasty, Tang Shunzhi (1507–1560), a famous general who fought against

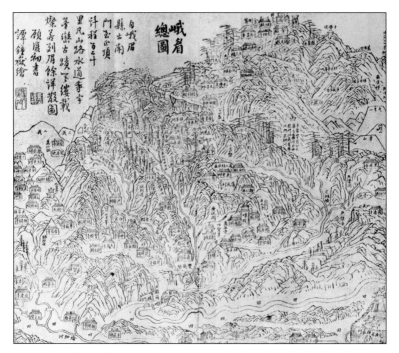

General view of Mount Emei, from *Annals of Mount Emei*, published in 1934.

Japanese invaders, wrote the *Fist Song of the Emei Taoists*, which gave a vivid description of the swiftness and flexibility of the style. At the time of writing, Emeiquan was improving rapidly and becoming more well known. The traditions were handed down by Pu En, a Zen master on Mountain Emei, and they are thought to have lead to the development of Shaolin martial arts.

Sichuan, the land of abundance, developed economically and culturally at a rapid rate, and frequent trade took place with the northern part of the country. As a result, Sichuan, Shaolin and Emei martial arts were influenced by other styles. Sengmenquan, Minghaiquan, Hongmenquan, Zimenquan, Huimenquan and Panpomen, all spread widely in Sichuan, are said to have originated from the Shaolin Temple at Mount

Portrait of Du Xinwu

Du Xinwu (1869–1953) was born in Cili, Hunan province, and graduated from Tokyo Agriculture University. He was an apprentice of Xu Aishi.

Song. Zhaomenquan and Shandongjiao are also thought to have had similar origins. However, many of these styles focus mainly on Duanquan ("short-range fist fighting"), and there are obvious differences between the Shaolin styles, which make more use of the fists than the legs, and those styles which have been influenced by Sichuan techniques.

Among the Emeiquan family, there are some local variations such as Yumenquan, Baimeiquan and Huamenquan. There are also some rare methods such as Hamaquan ("toad boxing"), Hudiequan ("butterfly boxing"), Panhuaquan and Huangshanquan ("eel boxing").

In addition, the Wudang, Nanquan, Xingyiquan ("shape-intensive fists"), Taiji and Bagua families have been practiced in Sichuan, and some of these have influenced Emeiquan.

According to recent statistics, there are 67 styles in Sichuan province with 1652 set patterns and another 276 exercises. Of the 67 styles, 28 are local variations in Sichuan, 27 are related to the Shaolin family, and the remaining 12 are related to other families.

Nanquan Family

Nanquan (southern boxing) originates from a hilly, sub-tropical region. With Fujian and Guangdong as the center, it is common in the area south of the Yangtze River. Legend says it was derived from Fujian Nanquan, or the South Shaolin Temple in Fujian, but no strong evidence to support this has ever been found.

Gongliquan performance by students from Guangzhou Yuanjian Girl's School, at the eleventh Guangdong Games in 1930.

As early as the mid-Ming Dynasty, wushu in Fujian province had its legends. Yu Dayou, a well-known general who fought against Japanese aggressors in Jinjiang, Fujian (today's Quanzhou), was a master of both the sword and wand, which was rare at the time. Another master of martial arts, Qi Jiguang (1528–1588), led his forces against the Japanese. Qi was born in Penglai, Shandong, and his kung fu belonged to the north Shaolin family. He taught the officers and men martial arts, and influenced the development of martial arts in Fujian and Guangdong.

Nanquan is characterised by its strict regulation, compact movements and emphasis on the lower-body. The forceful and quick Nanquan techniques require a balance between rigidity and flexibility, with rapidly changing arm and hand positions. It is fairly unique in this respect.

The Nanquan family took shape in the early-to-mid-Qing Dynasty, from the late seventeenth to the late eighteenth century. It includes hundreds of sub-forms, and these are widely found in Fujian, Guangdong, Hubei, Hunan and Zhejiang, as well as in Taiwan, Hong Kong and Macau. They

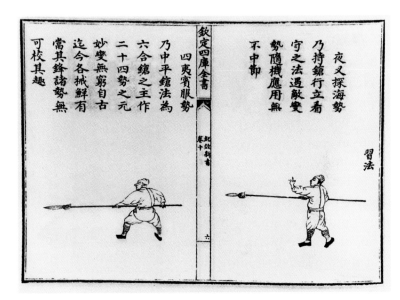

Two of twenty-four spear forms, from Volume Ten of *New Chronicle*, by Qi Jiguang. Ming Dynasty.

spread to overseas communities early, and took root in southeast Asia, Oceania and the Americas. In terms of contributing to the spread of China's martial arts, the Nanquan family is second to none.

Taijiquan Family

Of all Chinese martial arts, perhaps Taijiquan ("shadow boxing") most clearly displays the ideals of the Chinese people.

Taijiquan integrates fighting and good health, and requires a strong will and spirit. Its movements are guided by *qi* and require a balance of strength, rigidity and flexibility. Consisting of a series of spiral actions, with each action taking the form of a circle, Taijiquan noticeably differs from other families.

The application of Taijiquan techniques requires one's waist to be the axis that connects each movement. Movements may appear weak, but make use of great internal strength.

Based on the attack and defense principle, Taijiquan focuses on defense. It uses defense as the springboard attack: retreat can create an opportunity to advance. The underlying principle, "dare not be host, but be guest; dare not advance one inch, but retreat one foot", puts its emphasis on the weak overpowering the strong and the slow overcoming the swift. The greatest error is to lose control. It is a style that relies on philosophy and wisdom. It embodies certain Chinese ideals and the Chinese understanding of life and the universe. It can

Script of Separate Practice Method of Taijiquan by Wang Yueshan (pen name Songfeng). Kaifeng, Henan province, 1946.

therefore be seen as an expression of traditional Chinese culture.

The origins of Taijiquan have been long debated. According to the Li family tree in the Tangcun village, Henei (Boai, in today's Henan province), as drawn up in the fifty-fifth year of Emperor Kangxi of the Qing Dynasty (1716 AD), and found in 2003, it can be inferred that Taijiquan originated from the Qianzai Temple in Tangcun village. It was jointly founded by the Li family in Tangcun and the Chen family in Chenjiagou, Wenxiang district. The specific founders were Li Zhong of Tangcun village (1598–1680), the Li Xin (Yan) brothers (1606–1644), and Chen Wangting (c.1600–1680) of Chenjiagou. It was founded around the time of the late Ming and early Qing dynasties. After the chaos caused by war during the late Ming and early Qing dynasties, the Taijiquan of the Qianzai Temple was forced

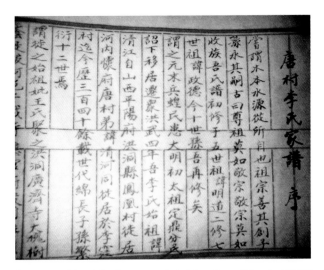

Genealogy of the Li Family, as compiled at the village of Tang in 1716 (the fifty-fifth year of the reign of Emperor Kangxi of the Qing Dynasty).

Chen Weiming in 1947.

Chen Weiming (1881–1958) was an apprentice of Yang Chengfu. He founded the Judo Society in Shanghai and wrote the *Arts of Taijiquan*.

to evolve into two branches: Li's and Chen's. From the beginning of the Qing Dynasty, Li's descendants taught in many provinces. The Li family tree demonstrates that Taijiquan was spread by relatives of the family. Chen's Taijiquan was different. Before the reign of the Daoguang Emperor during the Qing Dynasty (1820–1850), Chen's Taijiquan was only taught to generations of the Chen family. It was not until the late Qing Dynasty that Chen's Taijiquan techniques were taught to people from outside the family. With Beijing as the center, it subsequently evolved into three schools: Yang, Wu, and Sun. After this it began to spread nationwide.

Among the major Chinese martial arts, Taijiquan claims to have had the largest cultural impact. The combined focus on technique and physical health make it suitable for all ages, and it has become popular all over China in recent decades. It is now seen as a martial art with great momentum.

Xingyiquan Family

Xingyiquan, Wudang, Taiji and Baguazhang are known as the four major schools that focus on internal strength. However, the Xingyiquan style relies on strong attacks. It is therefore unique within the styles that focus on internal strength.

Emerging in the late Ming and early Qing dynasties, Xingyiquan was founded by Ji Jike (1602–1680), who was born in Puzhou (today's Yongji), Shanxi. It is thought that Jike studied for ten years at the Shaolin Temple in Henan during his youth, where he became especially skilled at spear techniques. Later, he developed fist-fighting skills. He believed in the "mind being the initiation, and form being the destination", and developed

Portrait of Lu Songgao, master of Xingyiquan.

Lu Songgao (1873–1961), the seventh-generation successor of Xingyiquan by Ma Xueli of Henan and also the founder of Shanghai Xingyi Quan.

Yue Fei seizing He Yuanqing. Tianjin, late Qing Dynasty.

Yue Fei (1103–1142) was a patriotic general of the Southern Song Dynasty. Famous for fighting the Jin troops, he also fought and defeated He Yuanqing twice. After surrendering to Yue Fei, He Yuanqing also fought against Jin troops. It is said that Xingyiquan was created by Yue Fei, but there is no evidence to prove this.

Xingyiquan, which is characterized by strength and swiftness, according to this principle.

Later, three distinct schools gradually devloped from Xingyiquan. The Shanxi school of Dai Longbang (1713–1802) adopted elements of Wuxingquan ("fist of the five elements"). The Hebei school was founded by Li Luoneng (1803–1888). Born in Shenxian, Hebei province, Li was mainly engaged in business, and the master instructor was Dai Wenxiong (1769–1861), the younger son of Dai Longbang. He developed the Santi style during a ten-year apprenticeship, which he taught to many pupils when he returned to his native Hebei. The third school was the Henan school of Ma Xueli (1714–1790), Dai Longbang's fellow apprentice. Ma was born in Luoyang and most of his pupils were Hui people. In the early years of the Republic of China, the two schools of Xingyiquan in Hebei and Henan spread to Sichuan, Anhui and Shanghai, and then far overseas.

The Shanxi school, however, did not spread far.

Xingyiquan is a pictographic style, whose main movements copy the attack and self-defense actions of certain animals. Pupils are taught to adopt the shapes and mimic the minds of dragons, tigers, monkeys, horses, alligators, chickens, snipe, swallows, snakes, eagles and bears. The movements of the Shanxi school are based on twelve animals, while the Hebei school focuses on ten. Both the

Portrait of Wang Xiangzhai.

Shanxi and Hebei schools use fists and palms frequently, but the Henan school focuses more on the elbows, knees, shoulders and thighs.

Xingyiquan uses powerful but concise movements. It is also influenced by Taoism, and emphasises internal strength training. In the face of enemies, pupils learn to summon huge strength and channel it into their attacks.

In the 1920s, Wang Xiangzhai, a disciple of Guo Yunshen from Shen County, Hebei, used Xingyiquan as a basis for creating Yiquan (also called Dachengquan, or "great achievement boxing"). The emergence of Yiquan marks a revolution in Chinese martial arts. Wang Xiangzhai gave up all the routines and tactics of traditional martial arts in favour of purity and simplicity. Yiquan has no routines or positions, instead encouraging responses as the situation requires. Wang used this style to fight and defeat other martial arts masters on several occasions.

Xingyiquan is characterized by simple actions, and has spread rapidly. The Xingyiquan schools are considered less conservative and are more committed to theoretical research. Today it is a popular style.

Baguazhang Family

"Baguazhang" literally means "eight-trigram palm", and refers to the trigrams of one of the canons of Taoism. The martial art is attributed to Dong Haichuan, who developed it in Beijing during the late Qing Dynasty. Born in Wen'an County, Hebei Province, Dong Haichuan is said to have been skilled in Luohanquan (a Shaolin-based style) in his early years. Later he learned various Taoist training methods in different villages, and synthesized all he had learnt to create Baguazhang. When he reached middle age, Dong settled in Beijing and began teaching students. A variety of schools quickly evolved. They included Yin-style Baguazhang, which was developed and spread by a disciple called Yin Fu (1840–1909); Cheng-style Baguazhang which was spread by Cheng Tinghua (1848–1900) until his death during the Boxer Rebellion; the two Song styles, spread by Song Changrong and Song Yongxiang; and Liang-style Baguazhang, which was spread by Liang Zhenpu (1863–1934), who formally acknowledged Dong Haichuan as his master at the age of fourteen.

Portrait of Dong Haichuan.

During the late Qing Dynasty and early period of the Republic

Portrait of Fu Zhensong holding the eight diagrams broadsword in 1929.

Fu Zhensong (1881–1953) was an apprentice of Jia Qishan, who was in turn an apprentice of Dong Haichuan. In 1928, he served as the master of Bagua zhang at the Central Guoshu Academy. He learned from others' strong points and founded Fu-style Taijiquan, which is popular both at home and abroad, especially in the United States, Canada, Brazil and South east Asia.

of China, the branches of the Baguazhang family took shape around Beijing. In the first year of the Guangxu Emperor of the Qing Dynasty, Guo Yunshen (1855–1932), a famous master of Xingyiquan, came to Beijing out of admiration. He and Dong Haichuan worked on the integration of Xingyiquan with Baguazhang. This work was completed by Zhang Zhankui (1864–1948), who combined both schools to create Xingyi Baguazhang. This style is still taught in Sichuan and Shanghai.

Baguazhang uses palms instead of fists, with circle walking its characteristic stance. This broke with many traditions, and opened a new door for Chinese wushu.

Weapons

Historical documents refer to the use of eighteen different weapons in martial arts. There is no overall consensus on the identities of these eighteen weapons, but they are thought to refer to the longbow, crossbow, spear, stick, knife, sword, lance, shield, axe, tomahawk, halberd, pole, whip, mace, hammer, fork and dagger. The weapons used in martial arts are quite different from those used by, for example, the military. People who practice martial arts fight alone, whereas military operations require the efforts of a unified team.

There are some strange weapons used in martial arts, and around 100 different weapons are used in total. The use of some of these has not been always been taught to new generations, and therefore the use of some is very rare. In recent years, the most commonly used weapons in martial arts have been knives, swords, spears, sticks and whips.

A weapon room. Stone relief, Han Dynasty, discovered in Nanyang, Henan province

The weapon room contains a spear, a lance, a bow and a shield. The figure near the bottom is the guardian.

Bronze Yue of the Warring States Period.

A yue is a large bronze axe with a long handle and a flat, sharp blade.

A ge.

A ge was a weapon used in ancient China. Used for hooking and cutting, a ge has a chiseled edge, a sharp blade and a vertical handle. The inner edge is used for hooking and cutting, the outer edge for pushing and poking and the blade for picking. In ancient times, ge and gan together went under the general name of 'gange'.

Short Weapons

The so-called "short weapons" are the light weapons that, if held upright, will not be higher than an adult's eyebrow. They are often held with a single hand. The most common short weapons are the knife and the sword. A knife may be single-bladed or double-bladed, and both are mainly used for cleaving and chopping. A single-bladed knife requires swiftness and bravery, while double-bladed knives require more skill.

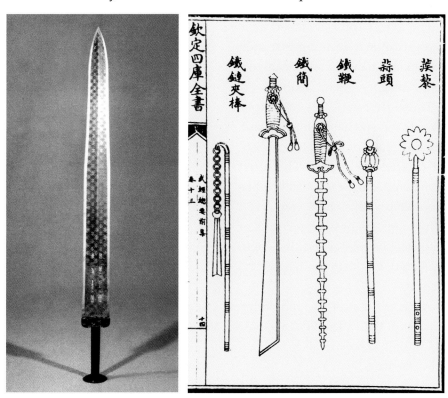

Sword of King Goujian of Yue State. Late Spring and Autumn Period, discovered in Jiangling, Hubei province.

It is 55.6cm long and 4.6cm wide, and bears the inscription 'King Goujian's Sword' in Chinese. It is still very sharp. Dazzlingly brilliant, it is considered the best example of a sword from the Wu and Yue states.

Various short weapons dating from the Song Dynasty.

A martial arts sword has a double edge, and is mainly used for stabbing. There are two types: the short sword and the long sword. Short swords are more prevalent. Some swords are decorated with a tassel (also known as the sword gown), and are display swords. Those without tassels are called military swords.

The axe is today classed as a short weapon, but in the past axes had longer handles and belonged to the category of long weapons.

There are two kinds of whips, namely soft and hard whips. A hard whip is made of steel and consists of thirteen sections. The most commonly known is a bamboo-like steel whip with a sharp end. A soft whip consists of nine sections of thin steel or copper rod. Its length is slightly less than the height of a person.

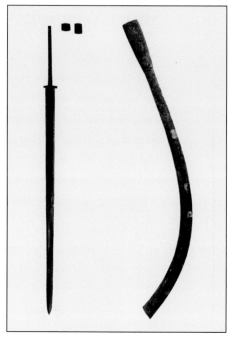

Bian Jing sword (left) and Wugou. Qin Dynasty, found in Lintong, Shaanxi province.

The Bian Jing sword has a flat stem and is so sharp that it can cut through eighteen sheets of paper with one stroke. It was still sparkling when it was discovered. It is covered with a layer of chromium oxide to prevent rust.

This wugou is 66cm long and has double blades. It can be used for thrusting attacks and hooking.

A mace is a steel weapon with four edges, but the edges are not sharp. With a length of about 0.8m, it is used for hacking and smashing. There are also double maces, and these are usually 0.6–0.7m long.

A hook is a kind of multi-bladed weapon, with a blade on its body and a hook-shaped end. The armguard is crescent-shaped, and has a sharp point and blade.

Canes are a kind of wooden weapon, and can be short or long. A short cane measures about 0.7m, and a long cane is about

1.3m in length. It is characterized by a horizontal handle near the end of the stick in the form of a "T". It is used for striking and smashing as well as hooking and pulling away the weapons of enemies. A stick resembles a cane but the horizontal handle, also in the shape of a "T", is at the far end of the stick. A stick is usually about 1.2m long and can be used with one or two hands.

A whip-stick is a thin, short wooden rod, about 1.3m long. It is said to have originated from a horsewhip. It is short, has no sharp edge and is portable and easy to use. It is quite popular in north-western China. There is also a short weapon called an "iron ruler", which is about 0.6m in length. Slim and without sharp points or a blade, it was popular in the Qing Dynasty but is now extremely rare.

Long Weapons

The most common long weapons in martial arts are spears, sticks and falchions (broad, slightly curved swords with the cutting edge on the convex side).

In martial arts, the spear is known as the "king of weapons". As the Chinese saying goes, "a spear thrusts in a line". Requiring a straight line in practice, there is a saying that holds that the middle horizontal thrust is the chief of a spear, which is hard to defend. It relies mainly on an outward block, followed by an inward block and then a thrust.

The stick, or "shu", has the longest history out of all the long weapons, and there are many types. There are long sticks, eyebrow-level sticks, shaozi sticks and many others. They may be made of wood or iron, with the wooden stick being the more common. The primary stick techniques rely on speed and power, and with enough space it is said that "a stick can hit a lot of enemies".

Xu Ning demonstrating the use of a brush-hook spear. An illustration from *Outlaws of the Marsh*.

A brush-hook spear has a hook on the blade of the spear head. According to *Tales of the Marshes*, weapons such as this prevailed against the armored cavalry of the Song troops.

The three-section stick consists of three sections of hard wood that are connected by iron chains, which make it flexible. A shaozi stick has a short, hard piece of wood at the end that is connected by a chain. The flexibility of these weapons makes them difficult to defend against.

A falchion is fitted with a long handle. There are various types, including the "spring and autumn falchion", the "reclining moon falchion", and the long falchion. During the Tang Dynasty (618–907), falchions were approximately 3m in length, weighed around 7.5kg and had sharp edges on both sides. Today, falchions used in martial arts only have sharp edges on one side. There is also another kind of broadsword whose handle is shorter than that of a falchion. It is long and narrow, and requires the use of both hands.

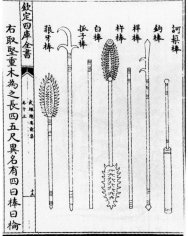

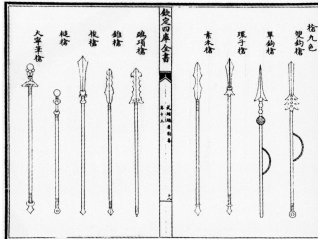

Various clubs dating from the Song Dynasty.

Various long spears dating from the Song Dynasty.

There are also some other kinds of long weapons. The "ji", or halberd, was popular before the Northern and Southern Dynasties, with variations including a long-handled single halberd and short-handled double halberds (a type of short weapon). The long-handled single halberd is divided into two types: the fangtian ji, with two crescents on the right and left sides of the end, and the qinglong ji, with a crescent on one side.

The fork is a common weapon which was used in the past by hunters. Types of fork include the ox-horn fork and the "three-head" or "triangle" (also known as the "tiger" fork). The techniques used mirror those used for the spear, and one advantage of the fork is that it can also be used to pin down an enemy's weapon.

The shovel is a rare weapon that can trace its origins back to a farming tool. It has blades at both ends, with the front blade shaped like a crescent moon; the tail is an ox-shaped handle with a blade at the end. The shovel makes use of unique fighting

techniques, and
was possibly a type
of Buddhist weapon
originally.

The rake is also a weapon that
evolved from a farming tool. A rake with
nine teeth at the end of it is called an iron rake.
Each tooth is incredibly sharp. They are usually
around 2.4m in length and weigh about 2.5
kg. Rakes are useful for both attack and
defense.

The tang, a kind of fork-like weapon,
is rarely seen in use. It has a sharp
point in the middle of one end which is about 0.5m
long. The other end has an outward crescent on which
a row of sharp blades are inlaid. The handle is up to 2.5m in
length.

Sword-shaped halberd. Mid-to-
late Warring States Period, now
in Nanyang Museum.

Chinese officials with their attendants during the late Qing Dynasty
They are holding bamboo staves, three-point steel forks and broadswords.

Hidden Weapons

Hidden weapons refer to projectiles or other weapons that are used for stealth attacks. The heyday of Chinese wushu was the Qing Dynasty, and during the latter part of the dynasty the gun became increasingly popular. Hidden weapons therefore became outdated, but some students still learn such techniques today.

Hidden weapons are divided into four categories: thrown weapons, rope-like weapons, shooting weapons and poisonous projectiles. Each category includes several types of weapon.

Thrown weapons include flying pikes, darts, flying forks, flying sabers and plum-blossom needles. Rope-like weapons consist of rope darts and meteor hammers. Shooting weapons include sleeve-hidden arrows, catapults and regular arrows, and poisonous projectiles consist of sleeve-hidden cannons, sprays and a beak-shaped pistol. Other hidden weapons, such as blow darts, daggers and gimlets, cannot be classified within the four categories.

The thrown weapons are the most popular and diversified among all the hidden weapons. Darts, also called hand-hidden darts, come in triangular, pentagonal and cylindrical shapes with pointed ends in the front. Each is around 10cm in length and weighs about 200g. A dart usually has a strip of red or green silk tied on to the end, called the 'dart coat', which is around 8cm in length and aids the flight of the dart.

Flying forks are made of iron and have three prongs,

Gold-decorated bronze trigger-mechanism of a crossbow. Western Han Dynasty, discovered in Linzi, Shangdong province.

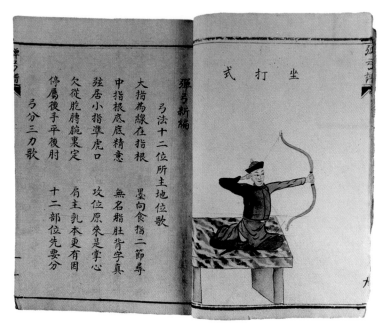

坐打式

弓法十二位所主地位歌

大指為線在指根　墨向食指二節尋
中指根底底精意　無名脂肚背字真
弦居小指準虎口　攻位原來是掌心
欠從脆膊腕裏定　肩主乳本更有因
停膺後手平後肘　十二部位先要分
弓分三刀歌

弧弓新編

Book of Spring Bow, published in 1806 (the tenth year of the reign of Emperor Xianfeng of the Qing Dynasty). Now kept by the National Library of China.

the longest of which being in the middle. The sharp tips of the prongs resemble spearheads. A flying fork is usually around 27cm in length and weighs between 250 and 500g. The fork handle tapers from the back end to the front.

Plum-blossom needles are a common type of hidden weaponry. Five steel needles, each around 3cm long, are connected together. On striking an enemy they produce a wound that resembles the shape of plum blossom, hence the name.

Rope darts, meteor hammers, the flying claw and the soft whip are the most popular of the rope-like weapons.

A rope dart is a steel dart that is tied to a long piece of rope. The darts are a little bigger than normal darts, around 20cm long and weighing around 300g. They have pointed tips and the other end is circular in shape. An iron hoop at the end of the

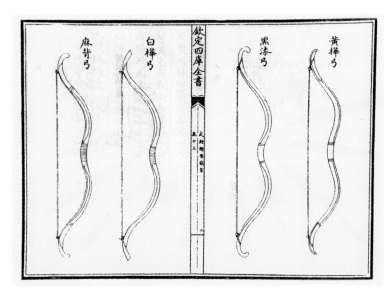

麻背弓　白樺弓　欽定四庫全書　武經總要前集　卷十三　黑漆弓　黃樺弓

Various bows of the Song Dynasty.

dart is used to attach the rope, which is usually between 6.7 and 10m long.

The meteor hammer is composed of an iron hammer and a long rope. The iron hammers are usually in the shape of a ball, melon or a ball with sharp spikes, and weigh 1.5 to 2.5kg.

Sleeve-hidden arrows are the most popular of the shooting weapons. They include single-tube arrows and plum-blossom-tube arrows. Both kinds of weapons are attached to the lower arm, with the front of the tube near the wrist. The tube contains a special mechanism. Only one arrow can be installed and shot from the single-tube type, but the plum-blossom-tube can contain six small arrows and can be shot continuously. One arrow is placed in the middle and the other five circle around it, to produce a pattern that is said to resemble plum-blossom. The arrow's stem is made of thin bamboo and is around 20cm in length. The tip is made of iron. Tubes that fire single arrows

Various arrowheads and bronze weapons from the Warring States Period, from the collection of the Tianjin Baocheng Museum Garden.

are around 24cm long in total, with a diameter of about 2.4cm. A small hole at the top of the tube is used to install the arrows, which are shot from a small hole at the front end of the tube. The plum-blossom type of tube is a similar length, but has a 3.5cm diameter.

A steel lotus, a kind of weapon.

The making of a crossbow, an illustration from *Tian Gong Kai Wu*.

Tian Gong Kai Wu was an encyclopedia of technology with illustrations by Song Yingxing (1587–1661), a writer-scientist of the Ming Dynasty. It documents many weapon-manufacturing technologies of the time.

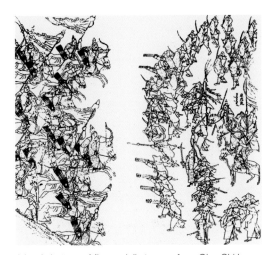

A battle between Ming and Jin troops, from *Qing Shi Lu*.

The Ming troops (right) used firearms as well as broadswords and lances, while the Jin troops were still using bows and arrows.

Catapults are also a common type of shooting weapon. They are made of hard wood and designed with a pod used to install an arrow stem. The crossbow is designed at the back end of the catapult and is controlled by the catapult body. Catapults are usually around 33cm long.

The sleeve-hidden cannon is the most commonly used of the poisonous projectiles. It is a special hidden weapon that requires gunpowder. The design has been adapted from the muzzle-loading cannons of the past. Made of bamboo, the pipe is around 40cm long and has three iron hoops on the outside. Both ends of the pipe are coated with iron; one end is the mouth of the cannon, while the other is used to load the gunpowder.

The Three Stages of Chinese Wushu Training

Over the centuries, wushu has developed into many different schools, each with its own training methods and techniques. There are, though, certain common disciplines. The exercises can be divided into three stages: refining spirit into *qi* ("visible strength"); turning *qi* into vitality ("invisible strength"); and changing vitality into void or emptiness ("refined strength"). Refining the spirit into *qi* is the first stage, one which attaches great importance to learning basic techniques, eliminating excess tension and developing strength. Refining *qi* into vitality is the intermediate stage and concentrates on the cultivation of "soft" strength and the nurturing of internal force. The final stage, refining vitality into void, refers to the exercising of extreme soft strength and the development of high-level mental and physical skills.

A description of wushu practices. Qing Dynasty, unearthed at Mount Yuexiu in Guangzhou.

Students begin by repeating basic techniques to gradually eliminate excess tension in the body and build up muscle. The stance, footwork, arm, waist, hand and eye exercises are considered an introduction to wushu. Once mastered, a student can begin the primary stage.

Refining the spirit into *qi* teaches students to use their natural strength rather than their raw power, which will lessen with age. The strength of wushu comes from the explosive power that is generated. Such power can hit objects as fast as lightning, and comes from key joints in the human body such as the shoulders, elbows, wrist, groin and knees. Joints and muscles combine to produce the strength of the human body, and students gradually

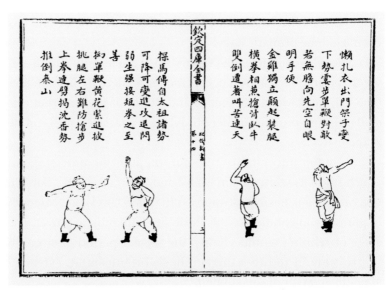

Quan Jing from Volume 14 of *New Chronicle* by Qi Jiguang, the Ming Dynasty
Created by Qi Jiguang, it is a simple and practical style.

learn to generate great power in limited movements. This power is commonly referred to as *cunjin*.

A key part of the primary stage is the learning of *Chaiquan* ("splitting-set exercises"). *Chaiquan* means to split the offensive and defensive movements from the set exercises and study the functions and use of the movements in combat.

After learning the basic techniques and several set exercises, students can begin to practice combining actions. This helps lay a firm foundation in hand, foot, eye and body exercises. Simultaneously, one can gather the *qi* scattered in the body in *dantian* to eliminate excess tension and increase strength. Once excess tension is completely eliminated, the body becomes strong and full of spirit and vitality. Movements then become steady, visible strength is achieved and the joints become more responsive. When a student reaches this point, he or she has completed the primary stage.

People who complete the primary stage are usually strong and vigorous, and have a keen eye. Sometimes, though, they are hot-blooded, unyielding, impetuous and proud of their martial arts skills. If they pursue further study, such characteristics can be refined.

Refining *qi* into vitality refers to the intermediate stage in which students work on "invisible" and "soft" strength. "Soft" in this case means flexible as opposed to weak. "Invisible" strength requires the integration of this flexibility with muscle power. The stage of refining *qi* into vitality, the second period of strength improvement, reduces the emphasis on muscular, "strong" strength, in favor of soft strength.

Refining *qi* is key to this second stage. Students learn to gather the *qi* scattered in the body in *dantian* during the first stage, but only now do they learn how to control the flow of genuine *qi* (*zhenqi*).

As strong strength gradually fades away over the years, the soft strength grows and the congenital *qi* (*yuanqi*) thrives. Those who master invisible strength are often clear-minded and energetic. If they encounter conflict, they are likely to react soberly and rarely respond with their fists.

One who completes the many years of difficult exercises that make up the second stage will acquire a deep understanding of martial arts techniques. Such individuals are often easy-going and lacking in arrogance; they do not attempt to show off their martial art techniques, nor bully others. Over

Li Jinglin performing Taiji Jian in 1930. Li Jinglin (1885–1931) was the vice curator of the Central Guoshu Academy at the time.

time, the exercises benefit the muscles, leading to improvements in figure and looks. The body becomes leaner and healthier, and movements become more lithe and graceful. The eyes also become sharp when fighting against an enemy, but at other times they remain clear and affable. At this point, the student has reached the stage of refining *qi* into vitality.

Refining vitality into void is the last stage of wushu. Exercises are designed to provide students with a refined strength. Invisible strength develops into refined strength via a state of extreme soft strength and flexible power. The higher level of strength does not exclude the wushu movements and techniques for attack and defense.

Refining vitality into void improves the reaction speeds of the human body. According to the traditional theory, the stage of refining vitality into void shall be done at the upper *dantian*, a round range close to "muddy pellet" (*niwan gong*); the stage of refining *qi* into vitality shall be done at the middle *dantian*, a round range in the rear of *zhongwan* and *jiuwei* plexus; the stage of refining spirit into *qi* shall be down at the lower *dantian*, a round range under the belly button. The exercise ranges therefore gradually move from the waist upwards. The key to refining vitality is to achieve "emptiness" and "quiet"; void refers to the modest inner center, while quiet refers to the normal mood.

Yi Lu Hua Quan, as transcribed by the author at Kaifeng, Henan province in 1971.

Those who reach the level of refining vitality are often generous, courteous and open-minded people. They are also likely to be gentle, elegant and free from worry. One who completes this third stage can be called a wushu master.

If an intelligent person was to begin learning wushu at ten years old, and proceed to learn without any interruption under the guidance of a wushu master in a healthy environment, then it would take around twenty years to complete the three stages. A wushu master is therefore usually at least thirty years old. The journey may take even longer. The age, experience and cultural awareness of the student will have a bearing on the time taken, and, generally speaking, middle-aged students are more able to understand the true essence of wushu and complete the long journey. Those who attain the greatest heights in wushu are usually over forty years old.

The Characteristics of
Chinese Wushu

As the offspring of the history and culture of the Chinese
nation, wushu demonstrates the characteristics and temperament
of the Chinese people. Wushu has its own national identity, and
differs strongly from non-Chinese combat techniques.

Systematic

Compared to other parts of China's historical and cultural
heritage, wushu is a large, independent and complete system.

Chinese wushu has many schools. Almost all schools take
the Yin and Yang and the Five Element Theory as the common
basis of their philosophy, and they regard "harmony between
body and spirit" and "harmony between quan and dao" as their
ultimate aims. In view of the theories on quan techniques, wushu
developed a system complementary to Confucianism, Buddhism
and Taoism. Certain exercises borrow ideas from traditional
Chinese medicine and the Taoist practices of maintaining
good health. Therefore, Chinese wushu combines philosophy,
medicine, the arts of attack and defense and the practice of

Shaolin monks practicing wushu.

maintaining good health to make up one large and profound theoretical system. This makes it unique around the world.

Other internationally popular combat techniques are characterized by speed and strong movements. But these combat techniques lack an internal element, instead focusing purely on the external (the offensive and defensive movements). Muay Thai, for example, emphasizes speed and strength, but offers no devotion to deeper theories. Karate, from Japan, evolved from Chinese Shaolinquan, and reflects Japanese ideals such as perseverance, ambition, valor and discipline. Boxing can be said to reflect the values of the Western world, including the enjoyment of exercise and the pursuit of stimulation. In contrast, Chinese wushu is characterized by gentle manners, the harmony of dynamic and static movements and the integration of strong and soft strength. The pursuit of these personal characteristics is common to many Chinese people.

Strict Order

All schools enforce strict rules regarding wushu practice. Students must follow these rules, and no shortcuts can be taken. Most schools teach courses that begin with basic techniques. Quan and weapon techniques are exercises meant to benefit the internal organs. It first begins with a series of external-internal exercises, a process of macro-micro level techniques, which are followed by internal-external exercises and a process of micro-macro level techniques, which completes the course. Once these steps are completed, students are able to integrate body and spirit and obtain both internal and external harmony.

The strict disciplines of Chinese wushu stem from the combination of ancient combat techniques and Taoist methods of maintaining good health. Karate, Muay Thai and boxing all depend on muscular strength and focus on combat, and although muscular strength is developed during the first stage of wushu training, the later focus on internal fortitude is what differentiates it.

The Gradual Principle

It requires patience and persistence to learn wushu. The journey can only be completed gradually and it is impossible to succeed quickly. Wushu attaches great importance to basic techniques and exercises, and combat techniques are rarely taught to beginners. The exercises which benefit parts of the body other than the muscles are considered fundamental, and the emphasis on maintaining good health (nurturing *qi*) and cultivating morals mean that combat techniques are never the priority. Such an approach makes wushu different to all foreign combat techniques.

Although they all have their introductory exercises, the combat techniques of Muay Thai, karate and boxing are taught at a very early stage. This allows beginners to master some combat techniques quickly. People learning Muay Thai can participate in a contest after completing just five years of training. This training includes basic exercises, practicing single moves and simulated combat. However, five years only allows time for physical strength to be developed. In Chinese wushu, this only constitutes the primary stage. If a Muay Thai student with five years' training fights a Chinese martial arts student with five years' training, the latter will probably be unable to withstand the former's fierce attacks. But if the fight takes place after ten years' training the wushu student is unlikely to be defeated, and if the combat is held after fifteen years' training, the wushu student would be the strong favorite. Students of combat techniques such as Muay Thai come to depend on physical strength, and are too eager to attain success. While some Muay Thai boxers make a fortune from fighting, their strength begins to decrease once they reach the age of thirty. Meanwhile, many Muay Thai fighters are injured during combat, and the healing process can be slow. A long career for a Muay Thai fighter, Japanese sumo wrestler or a Western boxer is rare for this reason.

The principle of gradualness determines the long journey of progress as beginners learn combat techniques. Because Chinese wushu combines combat with the practice of maintaining good health, practitioners tend to lead a longer life. Those who keep practicing the techniques they have learned year after year can prolong their life. Boxers and other fighters usually reach their prime between the ages of twenty and thirty, but wushu masters often do not reach their peak until the age of thirty. Some even peak around the age of forty, and their signature techniques remain unchanged even into their sixties, seventies or longer.

King of Yiyong Wu'an. This ink drawing dates from the Song and Yuan dynasties and is held by The Russian Museum, St. Petersburg.

Guan Yu embodied humaneness, righteousness and bravery. In 1123 (the fifth year of the reign of Emperor Xuanhe of the Northern Song Dynasty), Guan Yu was given the title of "King of Yiyong Wu'an".

Nurturing *qi* and Moral Cultivation

Chinese wushu regards moral cultivation as its foundation. It advocates nurturing *qi*, promotes the rule of law and emphasizes both civil and military ability. Aggression and violence are discouraged. Many wushu masters originally became students as a means of moral cultivation and

Zhao Yun fighting in Changbanpo. Mid-Qing Dynasty, Yangliuqing, Tianjin.

Zhao Yun was a famous general of the Shu state during the Three Kingdoms period. In this picture, Zhao Yun is surrounded by Caocao's troops. Black and blue pictures such as this where often commissioned by families after funerals.

health maintenance. Wushu schools always give top priority to ethics, and every wushu school has established strict regulations. Anyone who does evil or harm, regardless of their skill level, is unwelcome, and schools train their students not to fight with others, cause trouble or bully those who are ignorant of wushu. Instead, they advocate helping others for a just cause, wiping out bullies and helping the downtrodden.

Chinese wushu bases many of its exercises around the nurturing of *qi*. The aim of nurturing *qi* is to reach *taihe* (grand peace). The *qi* of grand peace runs in the opposite direction to aggressive thoughts. *Qi* is related to rationality, while *quan* is associated with law. The stronger the *qi*, the weaker the aggressive thoughts. The more the wushu learner achieves, the better his or her temperament becomes. Wushu learners rarely show off their powers. Moral cultivation and nurturing *qi* are the unique guiding concepts of Chinese wushu.

Aesthetics

Most set exercises and movements of Chinese wushu have an aesthetic appeal. The set exercises combine both dynamic and static positions. They are incredibly varied and are characterized by a unique rhythmic sensation and beauty. The movements of Chinese wushu rely on and make use of vigor, strength and speed. Moreover, the set exercises are difficult and require courage. Aesthetically, Chinese wushu is very diverse. Piguaquan, Bajiquan, Chaquan and Huaquan are fast-paced, elegant and masculine. Meanwhile, Shequan ("snake boxing") uses wriggling movements that are more feminine. Baguazhang and Taijiquan combine dynamic movements with static, softness with firmness, and a sense of both masculinity and femininity. Taijiquan is a particularly beautiful style.

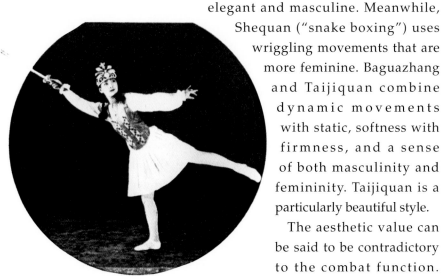

Film star Lu Cuilan performing a sword dance at Nanjing winter disaster relief meeting in 1930.

The aesthetic value can be said to be contradictory to the combat function. Many of the more practical movements of Chinese

Swordsmanship performance by
Luan Xiuyun from Qingdao in 1934.

wushu lack aesthetic value. During more than 2,000 years of
development, it has progressed from something simple to
something complex, and then returned to simplicity. Chinese
wushu was originally simple, with far fewer schools and
quan families. But a number of different martial arts schools
emerged and thrived during the Song, Yuan and Ming dynasties.
Wushu entered its golden age in the early Qing Dynasty. Some
Neijiaquan ("internal martial arts") such as Taijiquan, Xingyiquan
and Baguazhang emerged in the late Ming dynasty. Neijiaquan
uses small forces to defeat larger ones, and emphasises simplicity
over complexity. Its set exercises gradually became concise
and practical. Such trends also appear in the development of
many schools of Waijiaquan. Wushu development has been
characterized by a prioritization of the combat function over the
aesthetic value, which occupies a subordinate position.

Wushu is one of the most natural forms of traditional Chinese
culture. It has made its presence known on the world combat
stage with its unique combat techniques and training methods.

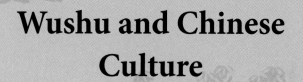

Wushu and Chinese Culture

As a pool of many centuries of human wisdom, wushu embodies Chinese traditional culture in martial art form. It also reflects the self-defense and health practices of Chinese people. The core philosophy of wushu draws from the Confucian principles of physical and mental integration combined with neutralization; the Taoist principle of dynamic balance; the Buddhist principle of cultural syncretism of Confucianism, Taoism and Buddhism in China; and the Eastern theory that man is an integral part of nature.

With the exception of the Buddhist practices introduced during the Han and Wei dynasties (202 BC–AD 265), wushu has hardly been affected by outside influences. Martial arts were traditionally the domain of the poorer people, and therefore can be said to reflect the character, thinking patterns and behavior of China's early working class. Therefore, wushu should belong to a purely civilian cultural class. Compared to the "elegant" cultures, such as music, chess, calligraphy, painting and poetry, wushu might appear hard and rough. At the same time, though, wushu maintains the simple and unsophisticated appearance of the country. It is famous for its robust beauty and is still considered a piece of pure land in the field of Chinese traditional culture.

Wushu and Regimen

Chinese wushu promotes harmony between body and spirit, and combines internal and external qualities. By nurturing a good temperament that fills one with vigor and vitality, and providing exercises to help one lead a longer life, it has long been considered as an effective way to maintain good health. Some also credit it with helping to build a strong immune system and preventing the onset of the frailty associated with old age.

Of course, good physical fitness does not automatically lead to longevity. Health is a complex issue involving a wide range of factors, but practicing wushu can be one of the factors associated with living a long life.

Wushu may keep one fit

It is widely accepted that practicing wushu may help build a stronger body, but the desire to maintain physical fitness is often motivated by a desire to improve one's external appearance. Wushu's role in maintaining good health is reflected more in the exercise it offers for parts of the body other than the muscles. According to an ancient Chinese regimen, "essence, energy and spirit" were the three key elements to living well. Here, "essence" refers to the essence known as 'Mingmen' that was traditionally thought to come from the kidneys and was considered fundamental to human life. "Energy" refers to the innate vigor that is said to come from the kidneys. "Spirit" refers to the idea that human nature and true minds are the outer reflection of "energy."

Portrait of Yan Yuan.

Yan Yuan (1635–1704) was a famous scholar of the early Qing Dynasty and one of the few versed in both civil and military affairs. He advocated practical usefulness, was opposed to boasting and founded the Yan Li School. He was also skilled at martial arts. This portrait was found in Taiyuan, Shanxi province, in the early years of the Republic of China.

Essence, energy and spirit are all said to be provided at birth, but are later reduced and damaged by various emotions and desires that come in later life. This leads to reduced vitality, disease,

The Martial Arts team of Henan Preparatory School, c.1920. Kaifeng, Henan province.

fatigue, premature aging and a shortened life. The Taoism culture of health preservation in ancient China stressed the need for humans to merge innate energy with acquired energy to restore essence, energy and spirit to their original state, thereby helping to achieve perfect integration and harmony between humans and nature.

Some consider the practice of Taiji to be capable of improving one's physical fitness. The balance of yin and yang is said to allow energy and blood to flow more smoothly and to prevent high blood pressure and many diseases. For example, the "nine palace and eight trigram palm" is believed to be capable of renewing cell membranes, enhancing immunity and preventing cancer. The Taiyi Wuxing Quan is said to help balance the functions of the internal organs, keep lipid levels down, increase lung and heart performance, and improve blood circulation. Taiji boxing, so long as it is practiced continuously and correctly, is also associated with helping to build a strong body, and the combination of Taiji exercise and energy circulation are said to

Yang Chengfu (1883–1936) performing Taijiquan.

bring overall benefits to human health.

Chinese wushu also includes many health preservation techniques, for example the exercise that translates as "stake skill for better health" in Xingyiquan. The aim of the exercise is to encourage both body and mind to relax. The practitioner becomes mentally silent and focused through a combination of pauses and slow, gentle motions. The process calms the nerves and removes feelings of chaos and tiredness from the mind. Simultaneously, it is believed to activate the physiological functions of various bodily systems and improve the performance of certain internal organs. It therefore keeps one both physically and mentally fit. Xingyi stake skills include dragon-like kung fu, tiger-like kung fu, ape-like kung fu and bear-like kung fu, and are suitable for the elderly and those with less physical strength.

A wushu master who has cultivated his or her mind and body to a high level will always maintain their peace of mind, and becomes more resistant to temptation and fear. They will never seek power or wealth, never be upset by gains or losses in life, and will never show off their martial art skills. The benefits of wushu, and its ability to nourish and purify the spirit, can be

Pu Yi practicing *quan* during the early years of the Republic of China.

The imperial family of the Qing Dynasty therefore placed great emphasis on archery, horsemanship and martial arts. Even the dethroned emperor Pu Yi (1906–1967) practiced *quan* at the Imperial Palace.

clearly seen in such masters. Physical fitness is the external effect of the training, while a peaceful mind and the power to master oneself represent an inner fitness.

Following the laws of nature is the key to longevity

The number of practitioners who maintain their vigor and vitality long into old age would seem to suggest that wushu can increase longevity. That regular practice can help prevent disease and prolong human life can perhaps be seen in the following examples.

There are some famous wushu masters who have lived to more than ninety, such as Yang Yuting (1887–1982), who practiced Taiji, Ma Meihu (1805–1924) and Liu Wanyi (1820–1918), who practiced

Xingyi Boxing, and Zhang Zhan'ao (1817–1916) and Wang Ziping (1881–1973), who practiced spring kicks. However, despite the existence of many long-term wushu practitioners, the life spans of some modern wushu masters have been shorter. Those who practice the same kind of wushu may not necessarily lead the same length of life. The Taiji master Wu Tunan (1884–1989) died at the age of 105, whereas Li Yishe (1832–1892) and Chen Zhaokui (1928–1981), who were also Taiji practitioners, lived for 60 and 53 years respectively. Human longevity depends on multiple factors, such as a person's economic situation, living conditions and psychological qualities, and these examples demonstrate that practicing wushu does not guarantee a prolonged life.

Ning Jiaokuan, a 96-year-old Taoist, demonstrating archery during the Shandong Guoshu Examination in 1934.

Mastering basic skills and turning brute force into controlled strength is the first step to learning wushu. Beginners must practice everyday all year round, regardless of rain or snow. Those who learn Xingyi boxing risk injury to their legs and feet if they use too much force. These injuries are often overlooked when young and return to affect the master as he or she ages. Moreover, certain kinds of kung fu skills, such as stake-kicking kung fu, iron-head kung fu and iron-arm kung fu, are more prone to causing permanent damage to the bones and muscles of students who are young, aggressive and eager for success. Injuries are all too common.

When it comes to practicing potential force and neutralizing force, internal energy grows and masculine energy is gradually weakened. Internal energy cultivation relies on individual contemplation and mental control more than communication with others. Masters generally teach their pupils more routine skills and less internal energy. Therefore, many practitioners typically develop their internal energy gradually, and in the exploration process detours and deviations are quite common.

Internal energy cultivation requires quiet and clean surroundings, as well as the concentrated spirit of the individual. An unexpected disturbance can easily scatter their energy, or even disturb the meridian system. When practicing the potential force or neutralizing force, therefore, inner injuries are more likely to occur from incorrect practice methods or accidents. Learning can cause dizziness or even high blood pressure if too much force is involved.

Wushu masters like to compete with each other. Many practitioners traveled through Jianghu after learning real kung fu and made friends with others by competing wushu. A Chinese phrase that translates as "making friends through wushu" refers to this. But injuries are common during competitions, since both parties regard the other as a deadly enemy and are fighting for

Buddist Arhat in Red by Zhang Daqian in 1944.

survival. Therefore, one must compete numerous times before earning prestige as a wushu master.

In general wushu masters are very competitive, and this competitiveness is often apparent as soon as a student begins to learn wushu. As a result, wushu masters are usually alert and ready to compete with others at any time and in any place. The state of being alert at all times means that wushu masters are in a constant state of nervousness, and modern medical science believes that the resulting stress is harmful and can contribute to both cardiovascular disease and cancer.

In summary, wushu masters do not necessarily enjoy a longer life and practicing wushu does not automatically lead to increased longevity. Nearly nine out of ten Chinese people around the age of one hundred are not wushu practitioners. But many practitioners benefit from living in pollution-free villages that encourage open-mindedness and shield inhabitants from worldly strife. This enables them to lead a thrifty life, without unhealthy habits such as smoking or drinking, or the stress of physical labor.

About Qigong

Qigong is also called Neigong or Lianqi. The term first appeared at the end of the Qing Dynasty, with Xingqi or Daoyin being used before that. It is a way of maintaining health via the regulation of breathing and the circulation of *qi*. Qigong is regarded as one of the more traditional Chinese exercise regimes.

Traditional Chinese culture can be considered a combination of Confucianism, Buddhism and Taoism. As a minor branch of traditional Chinese culture, qigong can also be divided into Confucian, Buddhist and Taoist styles. The Confucian and Taoist styles took shape very early, while Buddhist-style qigong was introduced to China along at a later date.

Confucian-style qigong is characterized by "seated meditation", with "quiet sitting" as the main form.

Portrait of Zazen.

Taoist qigong, guided by *Zhou Yi* (the *Changes of the Zhou*) and the theories of yin-yang and five elements, boasts a long history and has exerted the greatest influence. Given that *Zhou Yi* is the classic work of Confucianism, the Confucian and Taoist styles can be said to have originated from the same source, with each influencing the other over the years. However, Taoist qigong has been the more influential, and offers richer written works.

Buddhist qigong includes many sub-branches, with the most influential ones being Jingtuzong, Chanzong, Tiantaizong and Mizong.

Since the Tang Dynasty, Chanzong (Zen Buddhism) has been the most popular of the Chinese Buddhist branches, followed by Jingtuzong. After the Song Dynasty, Chanzong and Jingtuzong merged into what is now known as "combined practice of Chanzong and Jingtuzong". Jingtuzong advocates the pursuit of the western pure land of happiness, and is gaining in popularity; Chanzong highlights the power of understanding and is therefore popular among intellectuals. Chanzong qigong takes Chanding and comprehension as its major forms and zuogong (also called zuochan) is the most common practice. From Tiantai Mountain in Zhejiang, Tiantaizong advocates Zhiguan Famen, which is used to guide qigong practice. "Quiet sitting" is its major form, which focuses on the sense of *qi*.

Mizong, also called Tantra Yoga, was introduced to China from India as early as the Three Kingdoms Period, and spread to the Chang'an (now Xi'an) and Luoyang areas during the Tang Dynasty. It was later exported to Japan, where it became the Japanese Zhenyanzong style. It almost disappeared following

Restored portrait of Dao Yin. Western Han Dynasty, from Changsha, Hunan province
The various figures and brief explanatory notes describe medical treatment methods.

the Huichang Suppression of Buddhism in the late Tang Dynasty and the turbulent Five Dynasties Period, but was carried forward in Tibet and evolved into several branches. Mizong is closely associated with ancient Indian yoga, but it only began to spread beyond the Tibet area in the 1930s.

Confucian, Buddhist and Taoist styles are closely related, having influenced each other over a long period of time.

Qigong is seen by many as a science, but there is an element of spirituality or even sorcery to it.

The origins and early development of qigong are linked to man's self-aggrandizement. Since the earliest times, humans have dreamt about acquiring supernatural abilities. Ancient peoples were at the mercy of the laws of nature, and such aspirations helped them deal with their inability to control the natural world. Myths are thought to be one way in which early people challenged nature and attempted to make sense of the cosmos.

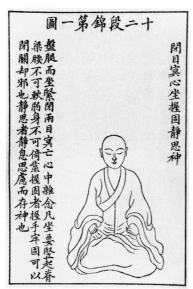

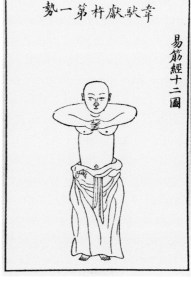

Shi San Duan Jin, from *Internal Work Illustration*, published in the eighth year of the reign of Emperor Xianfeng of the Qing Dynasty (1858).

The first formation of *Yi Jin Jing*, from *Internal Work Illustration*.

As civilization took hold, humans learnt more about the world and their delusions began to diminish. However, self-aggrandizement did not disappear; instead it remained deep in the soul, and has been passed down from generation to generation. Humans are still challenging nature, despite the many failures experienced and the great disparity between frail mankind and powerful nature. It seems that humans are powerless against their stronger opponent, but this does not stop them challenging their physiological limits. Two thousand years ago, Chinese Taoists began to recognize and develop their physical power with the help of many health-preserving methods, while Indians did so using yoga. The result was the development of what is now known as qigong.

Our ancestors found that qigong could give people unimaginable power. For instance, qigong can make the muscles of the body as tight as iron and resistant to external attacks. This kind of qigong is called Jinzhongzhao or Tiebushan in martial arts. It can also make a person more flexible, so that they can bend and stretch their bodies further. This is known as Tongzigong in martial arts. It can also make people more powerful, so that they can break stones and bricks using their hands (Yinggong). In addition, qigong can help to prevent diseases and maintain good health, which enables people to live a long and healthy life. This kind of qigong is called Yangshenggong.

Qigong can easily arouse the self-aggrandizement that is concealed deep inside human hearts. Human beings want to surpass themselves and to break away from all restrictions. Qigong presents a tempting opportunity to do just such a thing.

Human beings value life above all else. Chinese people have a profound understanding of this, and are consequently extremely dedicated to developing health-preserving methods. Traditional qigong theories state that, in order to exercise well, a person should first have a clear heart and mind, meaning no desire for fame or fortune, and that they should be quiet, determined and tolerant. Only with these preconditions may a person succeed.

Wushu and Literature, Film and Television

Wushu is closely linked to the idea of the knight-errant – the wanderer in search of adventures by which he can prove himself. The knight-errant story has remained popular for over two-thousand years, from the Pre-Qin period to the Republic of China era. The Xia culture developed around the Xia people (those who are adept at wushu and given to chivalrous conduct), with its core being tales of knights-errant.

Woodcut of Shui Hu Ye Zi: Song Jiang and Shi Jin by Chen Hongshou. Late Ming Dynasty

Many people enjoy reading these tales. However, rather than kung fu, they tend to focus on the characters' bravery, magnanimousness and determination. The heroes are trustworthy and willing to sacrifice their lives. Travelling without restriction, they break the bondage of mundane regulations and laws, and never bend to nobility. They dare to reveal corrupt officials. Often they live in the mountains or ancient temples, or appear in restaurants where they hold big feasts and drink and spend money recklessly. They fight hard against adversity and destiny, never revealing their love or enmity. They live a magnanimous life and choose to die solemnly.

The knight-errant complex is also a theme of many poems and operas. For example, it is mentioned in the *White Horse* (*Baima Pian*) by Cao Zhi (192–232), *Knight-Errant on Travel* (*Xiake Xing*) by Li Bai (701–762), *Farewell to Liang Huang* (*Bie Liang Huang*) by Li Qi (690–c.751) and *A Tale of a Girl from Lanling* (*Lanling Nüer Xing*) by Jin He (1818–1885). These works have been read widely. Many of these characters began to appear on television and in films during the twentieth century.

The chivalry of the Chinese people

Chivalry is part of Chinese culture. It concerns the resistance of ordinary people against the prevailing order, and also their longing for the perfect heroic character. Social injustice is the root cause of conflict, and this is the historical root of the chivalrous complex. As described in the *Water Margin*, "the Buddhist monk's staff cleared the dangerous road, and the Buddhist monk's knife removed all injustice".

This chivalrous complex of the Chinese people also contains a longing for certain personality traits. Research shows that in the historical development of a nation, characteristics that the nation lacks often become the lasting spiritual pursuit of many individuals of that nation. In China, the most desired quality is to be free from servility and obsequiousness.

Such novels do not reflect the reality of life, but instead present a fantasy world. Their world is one about which people dream. In China these novels are more like fairytales, and the idea of the knight-errant has been integrated into Chinese culture.

A new style of martial arts novel

Louis Cha (born 1924, writing under the pen name Jin Yong) has brought new vitality to this literary tradition. In a departure from previous works, his characters demonstrate masculinity and gentleness. He has redefined this area of Chinese literature and brought it into a new era.

Martial arts novels disappeared rapidly on the Chinese mainland during the 1950s for political reasons. Some famous authors also stopped writing. Despite this, Louis Cha became a success in Hong Kong and made his way to the top.

Emperor Xuande hunting. Ming Dynasty

The drawing shows Emperor Xuande (1426–1435) in Tartar costume while hunting in the countryside.

As well as Louis Cha, Liang Yusheng, Gu Long (Xiong Yaohua), Dongfang Bai and Wolongsheng (Niu Heting) in Hong Kong and Taiwan were also writing similar novels during this period. These authors and Xiao Yi, a Chinese author living in the United States, made up a new group, and their novels are known as the "new school".

These novels are fairy tales that are intended for both children and adults. Inheriting the artistic traditions of earlier works, the new novels focus on the inner spirit of human beings. The authors create vivid characters with distinctive personalities. The heroes usually have the emotions and desires common to all people, but at the same time each is endowed with superb kung fu skills. This type of novel integrates characteristics of both fairy tales and myths, and the books therefore beat a new literary path.

They can be seen as combinations of romantic novels and martial arts novels, and are often influenced by Western literature and film; emotions are highlighted, while wushu is indulgently exaggerated.

Each author writes in a different style, and the differences are easily identified. Louis Cha, Liang Yusheng and Gu Long are the most distinguished and influential authors. At least one hundred million people on the Chinese mainland have read the works of Louis Cha, and there are few Chinese people who are unfamiliar with the name.

The charm of Louis Cha's novels comes from the author's understanding of life, his deep historical knowledge and his unique writing style. His choice of words and his intelligent plotlines ensure the high quality of his work. Novels by authors who lack a deep understanding of life and awareness of history pale in comparison.

The works of Louis Cha often explore the conflict between personality and destiny. The heroes in his books attain perfection

Procession of Emperor Qianlong with Fragrant Imperial Concubine by Giuseppe Castiglione. Qing Dynasty

Giuseppe Castiglione (1688–1766), an Italian, came to China in 1715 to preach his religion. He also served as the imperial painter and left many paintings. *The Book and the Sword,* by Louis Cha, covers the story of Emperor Qianlong and the Fragrant Imperial Concubine.

in wushu and life. Nearly all attain their understanding of life as a result of perfecting wushu. Consequently, their lives become more admirable. The novels of Louis Cha often cover many years, documenting how the characters mature through their experiences. Louis Cha is also known for creating tragic moments. His characters often experience many difficulties. Many of these characters, such as Xiao Feng, Zhang Wuji, Hu Fei, Yang Guo, Chen Jialuo, Yuan Chengzhi and Di Yun, live with deep regret and unrealized aspirations. They often do not have the chance to put their excellent skills to use.

Cosmic iron sword.

Cosmic iron refers to iron that comes from "cloud stone". A bronze *yue* with a cosmic iron blaze was unearthed in Gaocheng, Heibei province, which dates back to the mid-Shang Dynasty. The sword in the picture is a modern one. Around 100cm long and weighing 4kg, the sword is sparkling with special patterns of cosmic iron. Yang Guo uses such a sword in *The Return of the Condor Heroes*, by Louis Cha. Taijiquan.

It is said, though, that heroes are born from tragedies, and Louis Cha understands this. By concentrating on tragedy in his books, he burdens his characters with heavy loads but also allows them to demonstrate their best characteristics.

Louis Cha's use of emotion is what really draws in readers, allowing them to sympathize with the characters in the story.

Wushu is similar to art and philosophy under the pen of Louis Cha. For example, the Baihuacuoquan of Chen Jialuo in *The Book and the Sword*, Tangshi Jianfa in *A Deadly Secret,* Shufaquan of Zhang Sanfeng in *The Heavenly Sword and the Dragon Saber,* Luoyingshenjian Zhang of Huang Yaoshi in *The Legend of Condor Heroes* and Anranxiaohun Zhang of Yang Guo in *The Return of the Condor Heroes,* are all sublime wushu deep in philosophical speculation.

While Louis Cha is considered the best author, there are others that must be mentioned when discussing great wushu literature.

Liang Yusheng (1924–2009) authored forty works, the highlights being *Ping Zong Xia Ying, Romance of the White-Haired Maiden* and *Heroes of the Tang Dynasty.* His protagonists are multi-talented, versatile and interested in literature, and he also includes historical elements in his fictional stories. Nevertheless, some critics accuse his novels of lacking authenticity and being over the top.

Gu Long (1937–1985) uses a very different style. He references many Western thrillers and uses a lot of montage skills adopted from films. Therefore, his works are more popular with younger people. Gu Long has written over eighty works, including *Handsome Siblings*, *The Sentimental Swordsman*, *Chu Liuxiang* and *The Legend of Lu Xiaofeng*. The use of short sentences and paragraphs is characteristic of Gu Long's novels, as is the creation of vivid characters and the use of large amounts of dialogue. He also uses the novels to speculate

Nan Jiyun from *China's Scenery* by Okada Gyokuzan, published in 1802.

Nan Jiyun was born in Dunqiu (now Xun County, in Henan) during the Tang Dynasty and was an excellent archer. He resisted the troops of An Lushan, but was captured after the county fell into enemy hands.

on philosophy. The works of Gu Long are fantastical, and this is one of the reasons for his success. However, his juxtaposition of sagaciousness and superficiality has been criticised.

Gu Long led a difficult life. For a long time, he lived alone and battled alcoholism. He died aged forty-eight. It is said that Li Xunhuan, the famous Xiao Li Fei Dao—a lonely and alcoholic character in *The Sentimental Swordsman*—is based on the life of the author himself.

Action Films and Television

In the 1960s, the knight-errant story became popular in Hong Kong cinema. In particular, Bruce Lee (1940–1973) took kung fu to a new and global audience.

Film still from *Burning Honglian Temple* (c.1928).

Film still of Wu Lizhu from *Guan Dong Da Xia* (1930).

Various performers and clerks from the Shanghai Mingxing Company (1934).

The actress Hu Die (1908–1989) in 1933

Xia Peizhen (1908–1975 - front row, far right), Hu Die (front row, third from right), the director Zhang Shichuan (1889–1953) (back row, middle) are in this photograph.

Bruce Lee was a kung fu master. His original name was Li Zhenfan, and Xiaolong was his stage name. At the age of thirteen he became a student of Ye Wen, a Yongchunquan master based in Hong Kong, and then went on to become a student of Shao Hansheng, who taught him Luohanquan and Tanglangquan. At eighteen, he went to the United States to study philosophy at Washington State University. In 1965, he established the first school of Chinese kung fu in the USA, and in 1967 he named the type of wushu he had created Jeet Kune Do ("way of the intercepting fist").

Huang Liushuang (1907–1961, nearest camera), the famous actress, performing martial arts in Hollywood, 1930

Huang Liushuang, whose ancestral home was Taishan, in Guangdong province, was born in Los Angeles. She became famous overnight by acting in *The Thief of Baghdad*. She subsequently came to China many times to shoot movies.

In 1971, Bruce Lee became famous by playing a leading role in *The Big Boss*. He then played the lead

Bruce Lee fighting Chuck Norris in *Way of the Dragon* (1972).

Film still of Jackie Chan from *The Medallion* (2003).

Film poster for *The Shaolin Temple* (1981).

actor in *Fist of Fury*, before taking a role in *The Way of the Dragon* and *Enter the Dragon*. As well as acting in films, he was also a director and a fight choreographer. On 20 July, 1973, Bruce Lee died from an acute cerebral edema. He was buried at a memorial park in Seattle.

Bruce Lee played the roles of kung fu masters who were dedicated to safeguarding the dignity of the Chinese nation. In each film, Bruce displayed his superior kung fu skills. *The Way of the Dragon* included the most wonderful action shots of all his films, and it has been made into an introduction film for learning Jeet Kune Do. In addition, it provides an example of a competition between Chinese kung fu and karate.

Five years later after the death of Bruce Lee, Jackie Chan became famous in Hong Kong. Jackie Chan was originally called Chen Gangsheng. He was born in 1954 in Hong Kong, although his ancestral home is Shandong. His was a poor family, and as a boy he was sent to the Peking Opera School run by Master Yu Jim Yuen. Here, he was able to learn martial arts, and within ten years he had become a kung fu master. At the age of seventeen, he became a stunt man and acted in Bruce Lee's films. After that, he changed his name to Chen Yuanlong, and then, in 1976, to Cheng Long.

In 1978, Jackie Chan played the leading roles in *Snake in the Eagle's Shadow* and *Drunken Master*, but he did not gain much success from these films. However, in 1985, he directed the film *Police Story*, which established him as an action star. Jackie Chan then went to Hollywood and became popular for his role in *Rumble in the Bronx*. He went on to direct *Rush Hour* and become the Chinese star with the highest box office value in Hollywood.

Jet Li (Li Lianjie) is another martial arts expert who has risen to action-movie stardom.

Originally from Beijing, he started to learn kung fu when he was very young. From 1974 to 1978, he won five consecutive National Wushu Championships and also participated in several performances abroad. In 1982, aged 19, he played the leading role in the film *The Shaolin Temple*, which was backed by Chung Yuen Motion Picture Co. The film, made on the Chinese mainland, starred a number of national wushu champions and demonstrated the true kung fu of China. It set box office records in Hong Kong and became popular all over the world. It also raised people's enthusiasm for learning Chinese kung fu. For Jet Li, this film paved the road to fame and Hollywood.

In 1983, action films *Wulin Zhi* and *The Undaunted Wudang* were produced on the Chinese mainland. The leading actor in the former was Wu Bin, then coach of the Beijing Wushu Team, and the leading actor of the latter was Zhao Changjun, a national wushu champion. Both films were very popular.

Crouching Tiger, Hidden Dragon, directed by Ang Lee and released in 2000, was a huge international success, and prompted a global martial arts film craze. The film is based on

Hong Kong film director Lau Kar Leung.

Lau Kar Leung is a famous martial artist, action director and film director. Like Bruce Lee, he uses real martial arts rather than stunts. The photo on the left shows Lau Kar Leung teaching John Chiang mantis boxing before a scene is filmed, while the photo on the right shows him teaching the actor Chia Hui Liu to use a three-jointed pike.

the story of the same name written by Wang Du Lu. Ang Lee incorporated the essence of kung fu and interpreted the classical Chinese aesthetic tradition and emotional concepts from a new perspective. The film won many awards at international film festivals, and won an Oscar for Best Foreign Language Film. In addition, the film also took more than $200 million in global box office sales, a record for a Chinese-language film. After that, *Hero*, directed by Zhang Yimou, and *Kung Fu Hustle*, written, directed and starring Stephen Chow, also met with great success, with each taking more than $100 million globally.

Hong Kong played a major role in putting kung fu on television. Many Louis Cha novels were adapted and made into television series. The most popular series produced in China include *The Swordsmen* and *Demi-Gods and Semi-Devils*, both of which received large audiences. Nearly all of the actors in both series were kung fu students. However, the popularity of the two series did not last. Because most of the actions were performed using stuntmen, the series lacked authenticity. This is a common weakness in television action series. Meanwhile, other series heavily revised the characters and plots of popular novels, which for many viewers diluted their historical and cultural connotations. Poor acting further diminished the attraction of some series.

Chinese and Foreign
Wushu Exchange

Wushu has developed as a result of certain encounters with other countries' martial arts. One such encounter occurred in the sixteenth century, during the Ming Dynasty, when Japanese Samurai invaded China. Another occurred in the early twentieth century, during the Boxer Rebellion. During these two conflicts, wushu masters began to recognize the advantages of other styles of fighting and the deficiencies of their own martial arts.

Two Big Challenges in the History of Martial Arts

Two major challenges to Chinese martial arts stemmed from conflict. The first occurred in the middle of the Ming Dynasty and the second took place in the early twentieth century.

During the Jiajing Period of the Ming Dynasty (1522–1566), a large number of Japanese samurai, known as Wokou ("pirates"), invaded south-east China. These samurai were fierce and merciless fighters. They colluded with Chinese pirates to attack and encroach Chinese prefectures and counties, burning, killing and looting wherever they went in Jiangsu, Zhejiang, Fujian and Guangdong provinces. For a hundred years, the government of the Ming Dynasty was forced to use its armed forces in response.

The Japanese samurai were accustomed to using the Wodao (a long knife), which is slender and heavy with a thick back and a sharp blade. Qi Jiguang, a Chinese military general and national hero during the Ming Dynasty, found that Chinese soldiers' knife skills were poorer than those of the Japanese samurai, so he trained his soldiers to use langxian (a utensil made of bamboo), lances and other long weapons. This resulted in famous victories against the Japanese pirates.

Competition between Shaolin monks and Japanese samurai is said to be the purest form of competition between Chinese and

Sword issued to Qi Jiguang's troops.

Portrait of Qi Jiguang

Japanese martial arts. According to historical records, Japanese pirates began a large-scale invasion of Nanhui (now part of Shanghai) in 1553 (the thirty-second year of the Jiajing era). The Shaolin monks led the defence, and utterly defeated the pirates. The Shaolin monks went on to defeat the pirates many times, although more than thirty monks sacrificed their lives for the country.

Most importantly, Shaolin kung fu defeated the long knives of the Japanese pirates. The power of Chinese martial arts was demonstrated against Japanese samurai, who had previously considered themselves superior fighters. This is a source of much pride in Chinese wushu history.

Drawing of battle array. Ming Dynasty.

More than 300 years later, China and other foreign countries became involved in another period of conflict. It began in Beijing at the end of the nineteenth century, and had spread to Tianjin, Shanghai and Tokyo by the time it ended in the 1940s. The period initially stemmed from Chinese resistance to foreign influence, and led to China becoming known as the "Sick Man of East Asia" due to the internal divisions and the series of unequal treaties into which it was forced to enter. The Chinese wushu community were united by a common enemy.

Although few have been verified, examples of Chinese martial arts being tested during this period are said to include:

Che Yonghong (1833–1914, Xingyiquan style) defeated a Japanese samurai in 1888 in Tianjin; Huo Yuanjia (1869–1910, Mizongquan style) defeated the British boxer Hercules O'Brien in Shanghai in 1910, before defeating a member of the Japanese Judo Association, also in Shanghai; Han Muxia (1867–1947,

Xingyiquan style), won a fight against Russian strongman Kang Tyre in 1918 in Beijing; and Wang Ziping (1881–1973) also defeated the same Russian strongman in 1918 in Beijing, as well as an American and a German strongman in 1919 in Qingdao and the Japanese fighter Sato in 1919 in Jinan.

Chen Zizheng (1878–1933, "eagle claw boxing") beat an American boxer in 1919 in Shanghai, and a British boxer in 1922 in Singapore; Sun Lutang (1861–1932, Taijiquan) defeated a Japanese samurai in 1922 in Beijing, and six Japanese samurai in 1930 in Shanghai; and Tong Zhongyi (1879–1963, Liuhe boxing), beat a Japanese samurai in 1925 in Shanghai.

Yang Fawu (no details for date of birth or wrestling technique) gained a series of victories over three Japanese judo masters in 1930 in Tokyo.

Ji Wanshan (born 1903, Shaolin boxing) won against a Russian strongman in 1933 in Harbin; Ma Jinbiao (1881–1973, Cha Quan) defeated an American in the 1930s in Nanjing; Wang Xiangzhai (1885–1963, Yi Quan), defeated Hungary Inge in 1928 in Shanghai and a Japanese samurai in the 1940s in Beijing; Zhao Daoxin (1908–1990, Xingyiquan, a student of Wang Xiangzhai) beat Norwegian Andersen in 1930 in Shanghai; Li Yongzong (a student of Wang Xiangzhai) defeated an Italian called James in the 1930s in Beijing; Li Raochen (1876–1973, Sanhuang Paochui) defeated a Japanese samurai at the end of the 1930s in Beijing and another during the 1940s in Nanjing; Cai Longyun (born 1928, Hua Quan) defeated a Russian strongman in 1943 in Shanghai and an American boxer in 1946 in Shanghai.

Due to the lack of historical data, very little information is known about the three foreign boxers who were defeated by Master Wang Xiangzhai. Hungary Inge won the world lightweight professional boxing title and worked as a boxing coach for the Shanghai YMCA. Keniqi Takuike, a Japanese master of five Dan in Judo and four Dan in Kendo, was also defeated by Wang Xiangzhai. After that, he began to learn Yiquan, and founded Taikiken on returning to Japan. Norwegian Andersen, who was defeated by Zhao Daoxin, worked as the bodyguard of Song Ziwen, the finance minister at the time.

Through the analysis of historical records, it can be shown that:

• Foreign fighters knew very little about Chinese martial arts and tended to underestimate them;

• Foreign fighters were defeated by Chinese wushu experts;

• These masters came from northern China, with eight coming from Hebei province. Three were from minority ethnic groups, Wang Ziping and Ma Jinbiao were Hui nationalities and Tong Zhongyi was of the Manchu nationality;

• According to statistics on Che Yonghong, Huo Yuanjia, Han Muxia, Wang Ziping, Chen Zizheng, Sun Lutang, Tong Zhongyi, Ji Wanshan and Wang Xiangzhai, their average age was 47.2 years at the time they first defeated a foreign fighter. Sun Lutang was 69 years old when he beat six Japanese samurai in Shanghai;

• Eight of the fifteen wushu masters listed here practiced Shaolinquan. Five used Xingyiquan and one studied Taijiquan.

Cai Longyun (right) with the author of this book in Beijing, April, 1998.

Guo Huide, who defeated foreign fighters in Shanghai in 1931.

At the time, foreign fighters who came to China were often arrogant and contemptuous. In the autumn of 1925, a group of Japanese judo masters gave an open challenge at Kunshan Park, Hongkou District, and Shanghai. Despite the Japanese masters' confidence, the Chinese master Tong Zhongyi defeated a Japanese samurai.

In 1930, Chinese wrestling master Yang Fawu also defeated many Japanese judo masters, which embarrassed the Japanese Mikado.

Chinese wushu masters thus achieved a series of brilliant combat performances that made the international fighting community take notice. However, some believe that the Chinese master Huo Yuanjia fell prey to a sinister plot. In 1910, the Japanese established a judo association in Shanghai. Many judo practitioners in Shanghai begrudged Huo Yuanjia his fame and success. They arranged a competition between Huo and some of the best judo students from Japan, but the competition ended in a brawl. Later, with his health declining, Huo was introduced by the judo instructor to a Japanese doctor who prescribed medicine for his condition. However, Huo's health continued to deteriorate and he was admitted to Shanghai Red Cross Hospital, where he died two weeks later. Some have speculated that Huo was poisoned.

Huo Yuanjia.

Born in Xiaonanhe Village, Xiqing District, Tianjin on 19 January, 1869, Huo Yuanjia was a patriotic martial artist and the founder of the Jing Wu Sports Federation. He defeated foreign fighters in Tianjin and Shanghai using Mizongquan handed down from the older generations of the Huo family. His life story has been documented in several films.

Chinese Wushu Goes Global

Chinese wushu has gone through three stages since the 1950s:

I. In the 1950s, the Chinese wushu community had little international communication. A few wushu delegations gave performances abroad when accompanying the country's leaders. In 1960, the China Youth Wushu Team and the China sports delegation performed at the second annual Czechoslovakia National Games, thereby starting the global exposure of wushu. In the same year, a team led by Zhou Enlai performed in Myanmar, where they were warmly received.

II. From the mid-1970s to the mid-1980s, the Chinese wushu community gave public demonstrations in various countries around the world. This allowed people to see and learn about its charms.

In June 1974, a Chinese wushu team was invited to visit Mexico and the United States. President Nixon met with all the delegation members and watched a wushu performance in front of the White House, which drew huge international attention.

In June 1974, the Japanese shadow-boxing delegation visited China, and in September of the same year the Chinese Youth Wushu team visited Japan.

Since 1982, and at the invitation of certain countries and regions, the Chinese Wushu Association has sent its best martial arts athletes and coaches to Mexico, Canada, the USA, the United Kingdom, Singapore, Australia, Italy, Thailand, Hong Kong, Macau and other countries and regions for assistance in teaching martial arts and setting up schools.

III. During the mid-1980s, the international community began asking Chinese wushu masters to attend international knockout tournaments and other matches. Chinese wushu masters are always challenged by foreign fighters when they travel abroad.

In March 1987, the first China-Japan Shadow-boxing Competition Exchange Conference was held in Beijing. Since the early 1990s, international wushu competitions have become increasingly frequent, greatly promoting the dissemination of wushu around the world.

According to statistics, Chinese wushu practitioners are challenged by Japanese judo and karate masters the most, followed by American boxers. The Japanese challenge the Chinese more than any other country.

China and Japan are neighboring countries separated by a narrow strip of water, and both countries have made cultural exchanges for many centuries. Japan's judo and karate were deeply influenced by Chinese wushu and have earned a high reputation internationally. In addition, Shaolinquan and Taijiquan are also very popular in Japan. Japanese people are known for their strong character, their diligence and their ability to learn from others' strengths. Many Japanese people come to China to learn wushu. In addition, there are many films of Japanese masters performing different forms of Chinese wushu, and many books on Chinese wushu have been translated into Japanese and published in Japan. By studying Quanshu (Chinese boxing schools), some Japanese boxers have been able to improve their skills. Some Japanese Tai Chi masters have competed against famous Chinese masters. Japanese martial arts pose the biggest threat to the dominance of Chinese wushu. However, recent Japanese teams have not been able to defeat Chinese wushu masters.

Muay Thai is famous for its violence and Muay Thai masters are very difficult to defeat. It is said that Bruce Lee, one of seven international combat masters, did not participate in much professional combat with Muay Thai masters. Thailand has sent Muay Thai teams to China twice, but both events have ended in their defeat. In August 2003, the Chinese team went to Thailand and defeated the Thailand team in Bangkok.

Vladimir Putin visting Shaolin Temple, accompanied by Abbot Shi Yongxin.

On 22 March, 2006, Russian President Vladimir Putin visited Shaolin Temple, where he discussed martial arts with the monks. Putin is a black belt in judo.

Western boxers are noted for their strength. To date, there are no historical records of the early fights between Chinese wushu masters and world boxing champions. Some believe that wushu and Western boxing have no apparent disadvantages in terms of fist fighting, and that it is difficult to say which is better. In the past, when fighting a Western boxer, a Chinese wushu master often tried to avoid the punch and moved with the opponent using nimble footwork. After outmaneuvering the opponent, the Chinese wushu master would attack and defeat his opponent. It is also said that if the two only fight using fists, the Western boxer has a greater chance of winning.

Taijiquan experts from fifteen countries performing Taijiquan in Xingtai.

On 3 November, 2006, Dong Zengchen, grandson of Dong Yingjie, a Taijiquan expert, held a martial arts exchange for over sixty international students in Xingtai, Hebei province, in memory of the 108th anniversary of Dong Yingjie's birth. The students came from fifteen different countries, including the United States, the United Kingdom and Canada.

Martial arts is an international sport. As well as Japan, Thailand and South Korea, many countries have their own fighting techniques. For example, countries such as France, Greece, Russia, Brazil and India are famous for their combat techniques. In particular, French leg attack techniques and Indian attack techniques have become world famous.

In recent years, Western martial arts communities have innovatively combined judo, karate, taekwondo, Muay Thai and Western boxing techniques, enabling them to display enormous strength in combat.

The exchanges between China and foreign countries in wushu have greatly increased since wushu became a global sport. More foreigners have come to China to learn wushu. At the same time, some masters in wushu have moved to other countries and taught Chinese wushu to students there. Their styles, skills and *qi*-promoting methods are now well known. This represents a challenge of its own, but it is a challenge for which the Chinese wushu community is well prepared.

The Development of
Modern Chinese Wushu

After the founding of the People's Republic of China, wushu became one of the most popular sports. It has subsequently seen great advancements.

In October 1949, the All-China Sports Federation was established with the approval of the State Council. In 1950, the All-China Sports Federation held a wushu symposium in Beijing, advocating the development of wushu and putting its development on the national sports agenda. In 1978, Deng Xiaoping also wrote the "good shadow-boxing" banner and donated it to a Japanese friend. The inscription is not only praise for Chinese wushu, but is also an inspiration to the world's wushu enthusiasts.

Established in 1952, the National Sports Commission listed wushu as a key event. It set up the National Sports Research Society, which was responsible for administering and promoting wushu and other national sports. In 1955, the Wushu Division was set up under the sports department of the National Sports Commission. Later the division was upgraded to the Wushu Section, responsible for national policy, the implementation of guidelines and establishing of competitions. In order to promote development, the Wushu Research Institute of the National Sports Commission was established with the approval of the State Council. In September 1987, the Wushu Section was incorporated into the Wushu Research Institute of the National Sports Commission. In May 1994, the Wushu Administration Center of the National Sports Commission was established, and this has overall responsibility for the administration of events.

In September 1958, the Chinese Wushu Association was established. It is a national organization, and one of the single event associations under the All-China Sports Federation. The Chinese Wushu Association is closely linked to other such associations around the world. Since the 1970s, a Chinese wushu delegation has toured five continents. Meanwhile, in order to promote wushu more extensively, the Chinese Wushu Association provides free assistance to developing countries in Africa, Asia and South and Central America to set up schools.

Modern Wushu Centers (Schools)

Wushu centers (schools) are important for its continued development. With strong government support, wushu centers have developed at an unprecedented rate. This has been helped by reform and the use of traditional resources. Currently, there are more than 12,000 wushu centers in China, with those in Henan, Shandong, Hebei, Anhui and Fujian being the largest and the most influential. Henan, a great wushu province, is home to more than 600 centers which are concentrated mainly around Dengfeng Shaolin Temple and the Wenxian Chenjiagou area (known as the holy place of Taiji).

Monks from Tagou School performing martial arts for tourists at the Pagoda Forest.

Students from Tagou School performing Taijiquan at the 2008 Beijing Olympics opening ceremony on 8 August, 2008.

At present, there are two major types of wushu center:

(I) Schools that rely on geographical and traditional wushu culture, integrating modern culture, science and technology education, and developing systematically on a large scale.

The Shaolin Tagou Education Group is undoubtedly a major representative of this.

The group is located at the foot of Songshan Mountain, and includes Shaolin Tagou Wushu School, Songshan Shaolin Wushu Profession Institute, Shaolin Wushu International Teaching Centre, Dengfeng Shaolin Secondary Vocational School and Shaolin Middle School.

The group has evolved from the Shaolin Tagou Wushu School, which was established by Liu Baoshan in 1978. Courses include routines, free-boxing, boxing, taekwondo and performance, and there are over 400 different classes. Non-wushu teaching ranges from nursery level right up to university education and beyond, with more than 28,000 students enrolled at the school.

Over the years the group has put equal emphasis on both wushu and non-wushu teaching, with the overall aim of improving morals, spreading authentic shaolinquan and producing new professionals. It attaches great importance to the all-round development of students. So far, its participants have won many championships both domestically and abroad.

In order to improve the development and dissemination of Shaolinquan, the group's performance team has been invited to teach and perform in more than sixty countries and regions around the world. The group has also performed as part of the opening and closing ceremonies of the 2008 Olympic Games and Paralympic Games in Beijing, in front of an enormous global audience.

Chen Shaolong (right) from the United States and Chen Shaobao from Britain practicing at Chenjiagou, Wenxian county, Henan province.

(II) Small, family-based and master/apprentice-based wushu centers which generally teach a single style.

This is one of the most ancient types of school, but they often incorporate many modern features. Many of these centers can be found in Wenxian Chenjiagou. At present, taijiquan has spread to more than 100 different countries, and taijiquan enthusiasts from all over the world become apprentices to wushu masters in Chenjiagou. Traditional wushu culture is merging with the modern tourism industry, with the centers offering pleasant scenery and the opportunity to live and eat with the families of wushu masters. Family-style wushu centers are small in scale, with food, accommodation and teaching all offered by the families of the masters. This kind of family-style centre only accepts a small number of students, and one-to-one tuition is therefore sometimes available.

As a result of increasing international exchange and cooperation, quite a few centers now run schools in other countries. Shaolin Temple is one such example, with centers in more than 50 countries and a total of more than 3 million foreign students enrolled. In 2004, the California House of Representatives passed a resolution to define March 21 each year as Songshan Shaolin Temple Day, so that California residents of all religious, ethnic and cultural backgrounds can enjoy Shaolin Zen Buddhism and wushu culture.

Wushu Education at Colleges and Universities

The inheritance and development of any kind of culture is closely linked to a country's education system, and for Chinese wushu to really become global, it must be incorporated into the Chinese education system.

In 1954, the National Sports Commission set up a competition for wushu teams at the Central Sports Institute (now Beijing Sport University). In August 1958, the National Sports Commission convened in Qingdao for the National Sports College President Forum. After the forum, Beijing Sport University and Shanghai University of Sport set up wushu departments, marking the formal entry of wushu into higher education. In 1961, the National Sports Commission experts prepared *Wushu*, the first handout for national sports institute undergraduates. In 1963, Beijing Sport University began to offer graduate programmes, marking a new stage of wushu education.

Since the economic reform and general opening-up of 1978, more and more colleges and universities have established wushu departments. The scope of these departments has constantly expanded to cover graduate, undergraduate, junior college, and correspondence programmes as well as ongoing education for coaches and various kinds of short courses for Chinese and foreign professionals. A diverse talent cultivation system has formed.

So far, more than forty colleges and universities have obtained the right to confer a master's degree in wushu. In April 1996, the Academic Degrees Committee of the State Council approved Shanghai University of Sport to become the first institution to confer a doctorate in wushu, followed by Beijing Sport University, East China Normal University and South China Normal University.

In July 1998, the Ministry of Education established an undergraduate degree called "national traditional sports". At present, the discipline mainly covers three main areas: wushu competitive sports, wushu culture and education. Folk sports and traditional regimen are also covered. For many years now, the colleges and universities that have fostered so many wushu professionals, carried out so much research and created such useful teaching resources have made a huge contribution to the ongoing development of wushu.

The transfer of sovereignty over Hong Kong from the United Kingdom to the People's Republic of China in 1997 has also allowed wushu education to improve. In the autumn of 2003, IVE (Chai Wan), formerly known as the Hong Kong Technical College, set up wushu programs, teaching mainly taijiquan along with other routines. This marked its first entry into higher learning institutions in Hong Kong, and had a positive influence on the further development of wushu in Hong Kong, Macau and South east Asian countries.

Wushu Competitions and Olympic Performance Events

After the founding of the People's Republic of China, the growing number of wushu competitions played a vital role in maintaining its heritage and promoting it in general.

Fu Shuyun (right) and Liu Yuhua demonstrate with swords at the Berlin Olympic Games in 1936.

Qin Lizi (in red) defeated Mary Jane Estimar from the Philippines to claim the gold medal in the women's 52kg free fighting category at the 2008 Beijing Olympic Games Wushu Tournament on 24 August, 2008

In September 1959, the first National Games was held in Beijing with 172 athletes from 25 provinces and cities taking part in wushu competitions and performances.

In September 1982, the Chinese Wushu International Friendship Invitational Tournament was held in Nanjing, involving 41 athletes from the United States, Canada, the Philippines, Hong Kong and China.

In August 1985, the first International Wushu Invitational Tournament was held in Xi'an. This was the first of its kind organized by China, and saw 89 athletes from 17 national teams taking part.

In October 1990, wushu was listed as an official competition event at the eleventh Asian Games held in Beijing. Some 96 athletes from 11 countries were present.

In October 1991, the first World Wushu Championships were held in Beijing. Over 500 athletes from 40 countries took part in demonstrations and free-boxing competitions. These championships are still held biennially.

In August 1993, the first National Wushu Hometown Competition was held in Wenxian county, Henan. The competition is held biennially.

In October 1996, the third Annual National Farmers' Games was held in Shanghai, and wushu was listed as a competitive event.

In May 1999, the first International Traditional Wushu and Stunt Competition was held in Taizhou, Zhejiang.

In July 2002, the first World Cup Wushu Free-boxing Competition was held in Shanghai. This competition is held biennially.

In February 2006, the First International Wushu Fighting King Competition was held in Chongqing. The competition is held annually.

In July 2009, the eighth Annual World Games were held in Kaohsiung, Taiwan, with wushu as an official event.

For many years, enthusiasts and supporters have been working hard to get wushu accepted as an Olympic event. It was a demonstration event during the 1936 Berlin Olympics, where the Chinese

Zhai Lianyuan attending the wushu demonstration at the Berlin Olympic Games in 1936.

Wushu Performance Group, consisting of Zhang Wenguang, Wen Jingming, Zheng Huaixian, Jin Shisheng, Zhang Erding, Kou Yunxing, Zhai Lianyuan, Fu Shuyun, and Liu Yuhua, were hugely acclaimed for their performances in Hamburg, Frankfurt, Berlin and other cities in Germany.

After the founding of the People's Republic of China in 1949, the government sent wushu delegations abroad to give demonstrations, with the aim of increasing its international exposure.

In October 1984, the Chinese Wushu Association invited the heads of martial arts organizations from twelve countries, including France, West Germany, Italy, Japan, and the United States, to hold an international symposium in Wuhan. Here, they discussed the further development of martial arts around the world and jointly signed a memorandum to establish an international wushu organization, to be led by China, as soon as possible.

In August 1985, the Preparatory Committee for the International Wushu Federation (IWF) was formally established in Xi'an. Subsequently, the representatives of the five member states (China, United Kingdom, Italy, Japan and Singapore) held their first meeting, electing Xu Cai as the director of the Preparatory Committee. The Secretariat of the Preparatory Committee was located in Beijing, and in October 1990, the IWF was established and headquartered in Beijing.

After the establishment of the IWF, the World Wushu Championships began to be held every two years. The first World Wushu Championships were held in Beijing in October 1991.

In October 1994, the 28th International Sports Federation was held in Monaco, and the IWF was accepted as a formal member. In June 1999, the IWF was temporarily recognized by the International Olympic Committee (IOC). In December 2001, the IWF signed an agreement with the World Anti-Doping Agency (WADA), and in February 2002, the 113th Plenary Meeting of the IOC adopted the decision to officially recognize the IWF. The IWF now has 120 member countries and regions in 5 continents.

Following Beijing's successful bid to host the 2008 Olympic Games, the IWF submitted in December 2001 the formal application to the IOC to include wushu as an Olympic event. Unfortunately it was unsuccessful, but the IOC did allow China to organize an international competition which took place at the same time as the Beijing Olympic Games. It was called the 2008 Beijing Olympic Games Wushu Tournament, but wushu is not one of the twenty-eight official Olympic sports, nor is it a demonstration event.

The competition was held in Beijing from 21 to 24 August, 2008. Some 128 athletes from 43 countries and regions joined the competition, and the Chinese team finished first overall with eight gold medals. It was a start, but wushu still has a long way to go to become an official Olympic event.

Folk Wushu Development

For thousands of years, wushu has been spreading silently and steadily throughout the vast land of China. Recent social developments have increased the rate of growth, with access to colleges and international competitions. Today, this traditional Chinese sport is changing rapidly, but the most colorful, dynamic, and vital is folk wushu. It is the basis of Chinese

Wu Tunan (left), a Taijiquan expert, and Li Ziming, a Bagua Palm expert, in Beijing on 10 June, 1984.

Li Ziming (1902–1993) was the Bagua zhang successor of the third generation and served as the first president of Beijing Bagua Zhang Research Association.

wushu, and the Chinese government has always attached great importance to archiving, cataloguing and maintaining these traditional forms.

In November 1953, the National Folk Sports Performance and Competition was held in Tianjin, the first of its kind to be held following the founding of the People's Republic of China in 1949. A total of 145 athletes took part in a total of 332 performances and competitions. The various disciplines included Chinese boxing, long weapons and short weapons, and the event served as an important display of folk wushu.

In September 1958, the Chinese Wushu Association was established in Beijing. It soon spread to other provinces and municipalities. The management of folk wushu is included in the responsibilities of the Chinese Wushu Association.

In January 1979, the National Sports Commission issued a memorandum on the preservation of wushu heritage. In May of the same year, the First National Wushu Exchange was held in Nanning, Guangxi. Some 284 athletes from 29 provinces, autonomous regions and municipalities, as well as Hong Kong and Macau, staged more than 510 performances. Traditional wushu began to appear in the official wushu domain. From 1983 to 1986, a country-wide survey of folk wushu and traditional wushu techniques was carried out that discovered 129 unique fighting styles and systems, 6.51 million words of theory, 395 hours of video recordings of veteran masters and techniques and many ancient weapons.

In early 1982, the first single-style research association, the Beijing Baguazhang Research Association, was established. Upon its establishment, the association moved Dong Haichuan's grave and tombstone to Wanan Public Cemetery in order to protect it. Later, it enabled various schools to catalogue their own Baguazhang techniques, set up tutoring stations in various parks to teach Baguazhang free of charge, carried out memorial activities to show respect for teachers and organised domestic Baguazhang competitions.

Since then, almost all of the schools of Chinese boxing have established research societies. For example, the Yang-Style Taijiquan Society, Chen-Style Taijiquan Society, Wu-Style Taijiquan Society, Sun-Style Taijiquan Society, and Xingyiquan Research Society can be found in Beijing, the Yang-Style Taijiquan Association is based in Shanxi, and the Jianquan Taijiquan Society and Chin Woo Athletic Federation are in Shanghai. These folk wushu organizations play a great role in the dissemination of knowledge and the improvement of health and fitness.

International wushu festivals and invitational tournaments have subsequently emerged including the Zhengzhou International Shaolin Wushu Festival, Yongnian International Taijiquan Association, Henan Wenxian International Taijiquan Annual Summit, Shanxi Traditional Yang Style Taijiquan International Invitational Tournament, Cangzhou Wushu Festival, and Shanxi Xingyiquan Invitational Tournament. At present, the World Traditional Wushu Festival is the most influential, and has been held three times since 2004. All of these occasions play a positive role in promoting the spread of folk wushu.

Development Trends

The coming years should be a prosperous time for Chinese wushu. It is anticipated, though, that the twenty-first century will also bring many changes. For example, larger-scale competitions and the weeding out and merging of styles are both inevitable.

Chinese wushu is unique in its integration of body-building, combat and aesthetics. It will undoubtedly retain its cultural traditions as it grows, and it will continue to follow its inherent laws as it evolves. Body-building, combat and aesthetics are the basics, but the prioritisation can vary. Between the 1950s and

Yang Fengtang (1896–1974) performing Xinyi Liuhequan.

the mid-1980s, wushu paid great attention to aesthetics and presented many new set exercises (mostly Changquan). Since the 1980s, though, wushu has prioritized combat and international exchange instead. Great importance has always been attached to the body-building function by the general public, as evidenced by the Taiji craze of the 1980s.

In the future, more importance is expected to be given to both body-building and combat. Chinese wushu will grow more quickly and become more practical under increased economic freedom. The aesthetic element will remain important, however.

Among various schools of Quan, the Neijiaquan (internal martial arts) is most vigorous. Neijiaquan closely integrates combat with body-building and exercise with health. Its combat techniques allow a small force to beat a larger one, and it has swept across the country within two hundred years. Compared to Baguazhang, Neijiaquan is

Cai Longyun performing Huaquan in Zhengzhou, Henan, 1983.

Cai Longyun is a famous martial artist and serves as vice president of the Chinese Wushu Association and assistant professor of the Shanghai Physical Education Institute. He is skilled in Huaquan, Shaolinquan, Taijiquan and Xingyiquan.

inferior in terms of aesthetic value. Taijiquan and Xingyiquan are similarly weak in aesthetics, while Yiquan has neither set exercises nor aesthetic value. However, those schools which put a lower priority on aesthetics are the ones that are spreading most quickly in the modern world.

Chinese wushu styles will continue to grow and evolve indefinitely. Its practical value will come to the forefront at the expense of its aesthetic value. The "dance" element will not be completely eliminated, though, as this is crucial to it entering major competitions such as the Olympic Games.

All schools are likely to face severe tests in the future. A large number of set exercises will become redundant, and others will be simplified or improved. Some schools of quan will find it difficult to survive these changes, whereas schools specializing in new combinations of styles will take their place. These will teach simple and practical styles, with more of an emphasis on combat than aesthetic value.

Changes such as these have always affected Chinese wushu. If it had remained untouched and unchanged during the last few hundred years, it would have lost its vitality and become far weaker than it is now. The competition and evolution that are a part of martial arts will always instill new energy and spirit into Chinese wushu.

Appendix I: Advice on Wushu Exercises

People who practice Chinese wushu usually aim to improve their physical health, but each practice session requires good preparation. Famous wushu masters are no exception. For example, people who exercise Xingyiquan often get pains in the lower back and legs due to the footwork involved, and Shaolinquan students are susceptible to foot injuries for similar reasons. People who practice martial techniques that involve the striking of hard objects are also prone to injury. "Internal" martial arts are associated with the central nervous system, and people should therefore pay attention to it when practicing this type of martial arts.

The following guidelines are intended to help students:

(I) Take it step by step. Rome was not built in a day.

(II) Never tire of repeating exercises. The more often you clean the net, the more fish you will catch.

(III) Choose one martial arts school and stick with it. The grass is not always greener on the other side.

(IV) Master the basic techniques, especially footwork.

(V) Drink a cup of boiled water after morning exercise.

(VI) Excretion before morning exercise is important.

(VII) Warm-up before beginning wushu practice, especially in winter.

(VIII) Cool down after wushu practice. Many students cool down by walking, but if you choose to do this then remember to wear something that will protect you from any cold winds.

(IX) Do not eat immediately after wushu practice.

(X) Feeling like the body is floating or sinking is normal when practicing "internal" martial arts. If you feel dizzy while practicing Zhoutiangong (a kind of internal martial arts), ask a doctor to check your blood pressure. People with hypertension should not attempt to learn Zhoutiangong.

(XI) Position training is very important, but avoid concentrating too much on this when you are starting out.

(XII) Equal emphasis should be given to the simple movements, including chongquan ("front punch") and tan ti ("front kick").

(XIII) Do not seek to learn difficult techniques straight away.

(XIV) Concentrate, focus and pay close attention to detail during practice.

(XV) Do not argue with your superiors.

(XVI) Do strike trees, walls or hard objects with any part of the body.

(XVII) Pay special attention to training that involves the groin, elbows, shoulders and knees.

(XVIII) Remain modest at all times, and do not resent anyone.

(XIX) Do not practice martial arts when tired, and do not practice internal marital arts at times of great sorrow, rage or joy.

(XX) Make sure you get enough sleep, increase your nutritional intake, and wash your feet with hot water.

Appendix II:
Chronological Table of the Chinese Dynasties

The Paleolithic Period	c.1,700,000–10,000 years ago
The Neolithic Period	c. 10,000–4,000 years ago
Xia Dynasty	2070–1600 BC
Shang Dynasty	1600–1046 BC
Western Zhou Dynasty	1046–771 BC
Spring and Autumn Period	770–476 BC
Warring States Period	475–221 BC
Qin Dynasty	221–206 BC
Western Han Dynasty	206 BC–AD 25
Eastern Han Dynasty	25–220
Three Kingdoms	220–280
Western Jin Dynasty	265–317
Eastern Jin Dynasty	317–420
Northern and Southern Dynasties	420–589
Sui Dynasty	581–618
Tang Dynasty	618–907
Five Dynasties	907–960
Northern Song Dynasty	960–1127
Southern Song Dynasty	1127–1276
Yuan Dynasty	1276–1368
Ming Dynasty	1368–1644
Qing Dynasty	1644–1911
Republic of China	1912–1949
People's Republic of China	Founded in 1949